Socrates

Socrates

Seán Sheehan

HAUS PUBLISHING · LONDON

First published in Great Britain in 2007 by
Haus Publishing Limited
26 Cadogan Court
Draycott Avenue
London SW3 3BX

www.hauspublishing.co.uk

A CIP catalogue record for this book is available from the British Library

ISBN 978-1-905791-10-1

Typeset in Garamond 3 by MacGuru Ltd
info@macguru.org.uk

Printed in Dubai by Oriental Press

Cover images: courtesy akg-Images London

Contents

The Problem with Socrates

The most dramatic story we have about Socrates is that of his final days. He was tried in 399 BC[1] as an enemy of the Athenian state, incurring a death sentence which he then carried out on himself. This act was an ultimate realisation of his philosophy. He argued at his trial that he was not guilty of the indictments – those of introducing new gods and corrupting the city's youth – and that he had always tried to live a good life. Nevertheless, he accepted the decision of a court made up of 500 of his fellow citizens, chosen by lot in accordance with the democratic principles of his city, and administered to himself a drink of ground-up hemlock. The scene was immortalised by Plato in his dialogue the *Phaedo*, and paintings by David and Dufresnoy confer on Socrates a dignity that contrasts with the agonised emotions of the friends who attend his last moments. Plato tells how an assistant checks the progress of the poison by feeling for signs of numbness in Socrates' body. 'Then he pressed his calves, and made his way up his body and showed us that it was cold and stiff. He [Socrates] felt it himself and said that when the cold reached his heart he would be gone. As his belly was getting cold Socrates uncovered his head – he had covered it – and said – these were his last words – *Crito, we owe a cock to Asclepius; make this offering to him and don't forget.* – "It shall be done," said Crito, "tell us if there is anything else." But there was no answer.'[2]

Plato's account of the scene was considered inaccurate for a long time because medical experts believed hemlock induced prolonged and excruciating vomiting, choking and convulsions. In recent years, however, this view has been challenged by a closer examination of ancient sources and medical facts. It now seems that Plato's account could be factually correct and therefore the calm and dignified death might indeed be an historical reality.[3]

Socrates' famous last words, referring to Asclepius, a god of health, have also been subject to differing interpretations – over 20, in fact, at the last count.[4] Ancient Greeks with health problems sometimes travelled to a shrine dedicated to Asclepius, spending the night in the temple of the god in the expectation of a divine visit in a dream which would lead to a cure. An offering to the god, in the form of a sacrifice of a cockerel, would be a customary part of such a ritual. It is possible that Socrates is being pious, reminding Crito of a genuine obligation they owe to the god; or perhaps he is indulging in a little black humour and trying to cheer the flagging spirits of his friends by suggesting that Asclepius will counteract the effects of the poison. Or perhaps, as Nietzsche first suggested, Socrates regards the hemlock as the antidote to the sickness of life itself and wishes to express his gratitude for this ultimate cure.

It is impossible to be certain what Socrates intended by his final words; and looking to his philosophy to support a particular interpretation only brings what scholars label the 'Socrates problem' to the fore. The problem is that there is no writing by Socrates himself, only accounts of the man and what he said written by contemporaries and later authors. There is no suggestion that he even wrote any philosophy. This dependence on others' accounts gives rise to the difficult task of differentiating the historical Socrates from his representations in literature. The problem was first remarked upon during the Enlightenment, and had become an established scholarly issue by the 19th century.

The Socrates problem confronts anyone interested in his biography and his philosophy, creating a mist of uncertainty

Aristotle and Plato from a detail of Raphael's painting, *The School of Athens*, Vatican Museum, Rome

that lingers permanently around him, but there are nevertheless some authentic and diverse sources of information for his life and thought. Plato and Xenophon are the two highly prized and yet very different writers – both ancient Greeks, one a philosopher and the other a soldier turned gentleman-farmer – on whose work above all we rely for most of what we know about the man and his philosophy. Both men, though, were about 40 years younger than their subject, so one cannot expect personal recollections of him from them before he was well into his fifties.

Plato's *Apology* is perhaps the single most important source for an understanding of Socrates. Written, uncharacteristically for Plato, in continuous prose and not dialogue form, it purports to be his eyewitness account of what the 70-year-old Socrates said at his trial. It contains no discussion of specific philosophical issues and so it is tempting to think that Plato's primary motive was indeed to give an accurate account of what happened to the man he deeply respected and admired. Other early works by Plato are generally accepted as reliable sources for Socrates' thought; and two in particular are key texts, both dramatising episodes in Socrates' final year. These are the *Euthyphro*, a conversation that Socrates engages in outside the office where he has been summoned to hear the charges against him, and the *Crito,* which takes place in the prison where Socrates awaits execution. Many of Plato's other writings that feature Socrates are more problematic and go the heart of the Socrates problem because of the difficulties in separating the thought of one philosopher from that of the other.

Very little is known about Plato's life. He was born into a wealthy Athenian family around 427 BC and grew up during the Peloponnesian War. As a wealthy young man, he probably did military service in the cavalry and at some stage he joined an intellectual circle where he came under the influence of Socrates. The effect of meeting and talking with Socrates was a life-changing one for Plato and in most of his dialogues, written after the death of his mentor, Socrates is the central speaker.

Xenophon, who lived from around 430 to 354, was probably in his late twenties or early thirties and was returning from a military adventure in Asia when Socrates was prosecuted and sentenced to death. He had seen Socrates alive for the last time before leaving on his adventure. His prolific output includes the four books of the *Memoirs of Socrates*, his short *Defence/Apology* (not to be

Xenophon and the Ten Thousand coming into sight of the Black Sea in Thrace after the battle of Cunaxa

confused with Plato's *Apology*), which overlaps with the *Memoirs* in its account of Socrates' trial, and his *Banquet/ Symposium* (again, not to be confused with Plato's *Symposium*) with its account of an address by Socrates. Xenophon was not a philosopher and he wrote much else besides the four works featuring Socrates. His chronicle of his three-year adventure as a mercenary, *Anabasis*, is the world's first autobiographical account. A very clear picture of his character emerges in this and other works. He seems to have been conventionally pious, practically-minded, didactic, naturally conservative and an interested, though never profound, observer of the human condition.

Xenophon, whose own character is likely to have affected his portrayal of Socrates, probably saw in the philosopher the kind of moral qualities that he himself generally admired. The Socrates he portrays often comes across as a banal thinker, worthy and pious but a little too morally wholesome. The dangerously radical philosopher whom others put on trial for his life is little in evidence.[5]

Xenophon's account falls well short of Plato's in this respect, but there is little direct contradiction.

Xenophon's motive for compiling the *Memoirs* is also a factor in his characterisation of Socrates, for he wants to defend the reputation of a man he greatly admired against the kind of criticism and defamation that led to his trial and execution. In this respect he was sometimes too successful, at risk of rendering Socrates an innocuous and rather dull person. However, while Xenophon is not a weighty thinker, he is no fool either, and being unduly concerned with portraying the virtuous side of Socrates, because of his indignation at the unfairness of the charges against him, does not prevent him creating elsewhere the impression of a very unique individual, one capable of winning his respect and admiration.

An experienced soldier, Xenophon was invited in 401 to join the forces of a son of the Persian king who was making an attempt on the Persian throne after the death of his father. Xenophon accepted, against the advice of Socrates, but his mercenary adventure, along with that of 10,000 like-minded Greeks, ended abruptly when the pretender to the Persian throne was killed in battle. The Greek soldiers found themselves stranded in Mesopotamia. They marched northwards towards the Black Sea and it was three years later that most of the 10,000 finally made it back to Greece.

Xenophon's depiction of the philosopher was influential for a long time and formed the basis of François Charpentier's *Life of Socrates*, first published in 1650. It was only with the Romantic movement in the late 18th century that the more ironic and opaque Socrates found in Plato was embraced instead. Amongst scholars today, there is still a pronounced tendency to underplay the value of Xenophon's portrayal, failing to recognise that Socrates might have been so complex as to appeal in different ways to different people. Xenophon's Socrates is similar to Plato's in his philosophical style, but this comes across in tamer contexts and without the artistry of a literary author like Plato.

Plato was born around the same time as Xenophon and like him was an Athenian, but he was also a philosopher who, as a young man in his twenties, knew Socrates for around the last ten years of the older man's life. It is from Plato that Socrates has come down to us in familiar form as the great thinker with an ugly body but a beautiful mind, a man who was sociable, convivial and not averse to sex, and yet morally compelling because of his overriding concern with the question of how best we should live our lives. Above all else, Socrates is presented as a talker, a thinker who thought and taught through the spoken word. Ancient philosophy was rooted in the oral culture of Greece. This is quite different to philosophy since antiquity, with its construction through writing of highly structured propositional thought. In the ancient world, reading was done aloud and when writing was employed it echoed the oral method, so that when Plato wrote about Socrates he usually did so in the form of a dialogue. These dialogues bring Socrates the conversationalist alive, while presenting scholars with the complex problem of differentiating the views of Socrates from those of Plato himself.

Plato was a great philosopher who can be expected to have had a far greater understanding of Socrates' thought than Xenophon. As a philosopher in his own right, however, and one who lived for over 50 years after Socrates' death, he continued to use Socrates as a character in many of his later dialogues. It seems unlikely that, so many years later, he was merely repeating what he remembered from his days as a young man conversing with Socrates. The fact that Plato is a dazzling literary artist in his own right, writing masterpieces in a dramatic and highly sophisticated style, complicates the problem of trying to draw a dividing line between his thought and that of Socrates.

The general view today is that the earlier dialogues of Plato are closer to Socrates' thought than works of his middle and later periods.[6] Broad distinctions between his thought and that of Socrates seem possible despite disagreement about the precise chronology of these works and hence of his philosophical development. For example, the doctrine of the immortality of the soul is one of the key theories of Plato's mature philosophy, known as Platonism, and in the *Phaedo*, arguments for this doctrine are put into the mouth of Socrates just before he drinks hemlock in prison. In earlier Socratic dialogues, however, Socrates keeps an open mind about what happens after death and is preoccupied with how best we should conduct our life here on earth. In fact, the doctrine of the immortality of the soul was developed through Plato's contact with Pythagorean thinkers and it seems likely that the historical Socrates held the agnostic views attributed to him in earlier works.

Texts of Plato's early period, those most commonly referred to as the Socratic Dialogues, include: *Apology, Charmides, Crito, Euthyphro, Gorgias, Hippias Minor, Ion, Laches, Meno* and *Protagoras.*

Texts of Plato's middle period, in probable chronological order and featuring Socrates as the major character, include: *Phaedo, Symposium, Parmenides* and *Theaetetus.*

Perhaps Plato, profoundly influenced by the life and thought of Socrates, felt justified in attributing his own arguments to the older man in his later writings because he believed that these arguments were the best philosophical elaboration and defence of his mentor's original views. This is a plausible explanation for Plato's use of Socrates in propounding his theory of Forms, the second key doctrine of Platonism. One characteristic of Socrates' thought that emerges from all the major sources is the idea of exploring an ethical concept by looking at possible definitions of the term under discussion. You cannot hope to proceed with an ethical question about, for example, how best to conduct your life justly without first having some awareness of what justness is. The idea that there could be a fixed definition of a concept, one that people could agree to recognise despite their other philosophical differences, led

Plato to believe that a thing like justice might really exist. If it does not exist, one might ask, what is the point in trying to define it? Such reasoning, although never suggested by Socrates in the early dialogues, resulted in the theory that Plato is now most famous for, the theory that concepts like justice are not just ideas in our minds but independently existing Forms of an unchangeable nature. Such a full-blown theory could be ascribed to Socrates because it could be seen as a development of his insistence on the need to try and establish definitions, even though Socrates never advanced such a theory himself and never obtained, or thought he could obtain, satisfactory definitions.

Plato left Athens after Socrates' execution and traveled widely before returning to the city 12 years later. He set up his Academy, named after the grove of Akademos in which it was situated, and set about instructing the young through a general course in philosophy, mathematics and logic. We do not know for certain why Plato left Athens, but the manner of Socrates' death is likely to have played a part in that decision.

This view may be particularly charitable to Plato, though it is broadly in line with the way in which Socrates becomes less of an individual voice in his later dialogues and by the time of his very late works has virtually disappeared altogether. Another way of putting the relationship between the two philosophers is that at some point around the middle period of Plato's development, in dialogues like *Symposium* and *Phaedo*, Plato stops being a Socratic thinker and the figure of Socrates in his dialogues becomes a Platonic thinker. The Socrates of the later Plato has a magisterial theory to propound, but the early Socrates of Plato is not concerned with teaching a set of ideas; indeed, he disavows the role of teacher.

Strong supporting evidence for the idea that the theory of Forms belongs firmly to Plato and not Socrates comes from the philosopher Aristotle. He was born 15 years after the death of Socrates, so did not share the personal acquaintance or emotional involvement with Socrates so important to Xenophon's and Plato's accounts, but he joined Plato's Academy as a teenage student and remained there for 20 years. He would have had unique opportunities to ponder the question that bedevils the search for the historical Socrates, namely the relationship between the philosophies of Plato and Socrates. His conclusion, stated dispassionately and unambiguously, is that Socrates was the first to concentrate on definitions and that this influenced Plato, who 'came to the conclusion that the universal belonged to a different world from the world of sense-perception'.[7]

The theory of Forms as propounded by Socrates in the works of Plato presents us as afflicted by an unstable and fluctuating sense of reality. All that we see as beautiful, for example, is an illusion because the true reality of Beauty is only apprehensible through our intellect. The material world is only a pale imitation of the Forms.

As well as the accounts by Plato and Xenophon, both written after the philosopher's death, there is a dramatic portrait of Socrates written, uniquely, when he was still alive. It comes from a comedy by the playwright Aristophanes, *Clouds*, which was first produced in 423, when Socrates was in his mid-forties. The play was performed at the Great Dionysia, the main dramatic festival and competition in Athens, and in keeping with the genre of 5th-century Athenian comedy, the drama is built around farce, sexual humour, satire and comic irreverence. The plays of Aristophanes are a cultural barometer of their times, sensitive to social strains and anxieties while exploring them through caricature and satire to the point of fantasy, and prominent men in the life of the city are key targets for his humour and burlesque routines.

In *Clouds*, it is clear that Socrates was a recognisable character in Athens at the time and that he was associated with a group of teachers who were known for their teaching of rhetorical skills. Traditionalists regarded these teachers with suspicion for they seemed to be undermining conventional ways of thinking. Learned disagreement continues as to the nature of the playwright's attitude towards Socrates and, given the genre's conventions and the fact that Aristophanes appears as a friend of the philosopher in Plato's *Symposium*, it is not necessarily as personally hostile as at first might appear.

The fact that the four main sources for Socrates – Xenophon, Plato, Aristotle and Aristophanes – are not always in agreement is not always the biographical calamity that might be feared. The two philosophers, the retired soldier and the playwright are four very different individuals, each with his own perspective on Socrates, and together they provide a rich and authentic set of sources, especially because there are features that overlap in their accounts. There is also a multitude of evidence that comes from a variety of other, less reliable, sources. There are scattered references from 4th-century orators, a biography of Socrates written by an author known as Diogenes Laertius around AD 200, and a host of anecdotes and impressions from later writers, including renowned figures like Cicero and Plutarch as well as obscure Christian writers. Some or all of these may have had access to reliable sources of information that have not survived, although, with no sure way of knowing this, a healthy dose of circumspection is warranted.[9]

What emerges from the disparate sources as a whole is a clear indication of the tremendous impact that Socrates made on very different people, both as an individual personality and as a philosophical voice. What also emerges is the possibility that the Socrates problem goes deeper than the indeterminate nature of

'Two things may properly be ascribed to Socrates, inductive reasoning and definition by universals – both belonging to the very fundamentals of science. But Socrates did not assign to the universal or the definitions an independent existence. It was the others who made them separate, and called these separate entities the Forms of everything that exists.'

Aristotle, *Metaphysics*.[8]

the sources and the uncertain course of Plato's philosophical development. It seems that, even were we to discover a papyrus in the sands of North Africa bearing writing by Socrates himself, the enigma would remain because there was an irreducible, riddling complexity to the man. To the hardened soldier Xenophon he is a loyal and upright citizen who exhibits admirable moral qualities; to Plato, a profound thinker after whom it has been said all subsequent Western philosophy is a footnote, Socrates is a witty and disturbing intellectual who changes the way we look at ourselves and the world; to the comic playwright Aristophanes he is an eccentric and unworldly Athenian; and, to the polymath Aristotle, the 'melancholic' Socrates is the man who set Plato off on his philosophical journey.[10]

The intriguing and ambiguous nature of Socrates reveals itself in a number of anecdotes, too many to ignore altogether. Cicero, using a probably reliable source, tells how a certain Zopyrus, claiming knowledge of physiognomy but not knowing who Socrates was, read in his face that he was full of vices and a lustful womaniser.[11] The rest of the company present laughed aloud at this interpretation but Socrates concurred, agreeing that such propensities were indeed in his nature but that he had learned to master them. The suggestion here of a mental concentration strong enough to rein in a potentially disruptive sexual energy is confirmed by another story in Plato's *Symposium*, told by Alcibiades, a friend of Socrates.

Alcibiades tells how, when they were soldiers together on a campaign in the northern Aegean, Socrates 'started thinking about some problem or other; he just stood outside trying to figure it out. He couldn't resolve it, but he wouldn't give up. He simply stood there, glued to the same spot. By midday, many soldiers had seen him, and, quite mystified, they told everyone that Socrates was still standing there when evening came. After dinner some Ionian soldiers moved their bedding outside, where it was cooler and more comfortable (all this took place in the summer), but mainly in order to watch if Socrates was going to stay out there all night. And so he did; he stood there on the very same spot until dawn! He only left next morning, when the sun came out, and he made his prayers to the new day.'[12] This goes well beyond the stereotyped image of the absent-minded professor: it suggests a state of meditation like that achieved by Buddhist monks, which, if the story is true, would require supreme powers of concentration.

Vases of the early 6th century depict the hirsute Silenus intent on the pursuit of Nymphs; and sometimes the wine god Dionysus appears with him. Silenus indulges in carnivalesque frolics and enjoys the pleasure of wine and dance while he accompanies the tipsy god on some of his adventures. A contrary kind of association links Silenus with hidden knowledge and wisdom and there are legends of attempts to capture him so that his secret knowledge can be shared.

At the end of the *Symposium*, Alcibiades compares him to certain little statues of Silenus, a mythical creature whose semi-human form is characterised by a bald head, pot belly, pug nose, large ears and a horse's tail. These little statues contained still smaller statues hidden inside them, like Russian dolls. The Socrates we think we are viewing is only a mask or shell, behind which there lies another possible Socrates. There may be still further shells beneath. Alcibiades is acknowledging the difficulty of knowing Socrates and the likelihood that the familiar figure of the philosopher hides another identity. Moreover, the comparison with Silenus, who was often associated with the satyrs because of his bestial nature and behaviour, echoes the passage from Cicero in which the face reader discerns a lascivious sensualist in Socrates.

Alcibiades is aware too of the way Socrates conceals himself behind a mask of irony, with a teasing ability to question and unsettle others by following through the logic of their arguments without revealing any agenda of his own. He pretends to be a simplistic buffoon, says Alcibiades, but 'his whole life is one big game — a game of irony'.[13] Socrates interrogates, but without threats; skilfully and clinically, as if innocuously, he reveals his interlocutors' ignorance and so creates an opportunity for them to discover new wisdom. Alcibiades describes how Socrates proceeds by returning to the analogy with the little statues of Silenus: 'He's always going on about pack asses, or blacksmiths, or cobblers, or tanners; he's always making the same tired old points in the same tired old words. If you are foolish or simply unfamiliar with him, you'd find it impossible not to laugh at his arguments. But if you see them when they open up like the statues, if you go behind their surface, you'll realise that no other arguments make any sense.'[14]

This is a more familiar picture of Socrates the intellectual, exquisitely rational in his ability to tease out an argument, but it sits uneasily alongside another aspect of his behaviour. Both Plato and Xenophon refer a number of times to what Socrates called his divine sign (*daimonion*), an inexplicable occurrence that comes to him unbidden: *This began when I was a child. It is a voice, and whenever it speaks it turns me away from something I am going to do, but it never encourages me to do anything.*[15] Both Plato and Xenophon link these episodes to one of the charges that brought about his death sentence, that of introducing new gods to Athens. Socrates' divine sign points to an introspective and non-rational side to the philosopher, further complicating our picture of him. Socrates the sophisticated rationalist, cerebral and logical, is also Socrates the intuitive, possibly mystical, thinker capable of trance-like meditative states.[16]

It is revealing to compare the case of Socrates with that of Shakespeare, another iconic cultural figure whose person we can discern only indirectly, an ambiguous presence in the shadows of the texts with which he is associated. Socrates is even more obscure than Shakespeare because there are no texts in his own name and the historical Socrates of Plato is bound up with the fictional character of Plato's art. With Shakespeare, too, we can trace a growing maturity between the early and late plays, but Socrates emerges in the sources as fully formed, philosophically unified in his insistence that what matters is how we live, caring for our selves and looking after our souls.

The Socrates problem, then, takes several forms. It is part of the fascination of a man who wrote nothing but argued himself into a death sentence. Socrates seems strange because he has so many faces: he is an intellectual, an ironist, a sensualist, a soldier, a citizen and a mystic, and this complex, potent mix is also a part of the problem of coming to understand him. 'Even if I were to imagine myself his contemporary', wrote Kierkegaard, 'he would still always be difficult to comprehend.'[17] It was Kierkegaard who realised that the varying accounts and interpretations of Socrates through the ages point to a mystery at the heart of the man and that, paradoxically, the Socrates who is famous for his talking is really a silent figure. This very inscrutability is alluring in itself.

'Socrates' life is like a magnificent pause in the course of history: we do not hear him at all; a profound stillness prevails – until it is broken by the noisy attempts of the many and different schools of followers to trace their origin in this hidden and cryptic source.'

Kierkegaard, *The Concept of Irony*.[18]

There are also strange aspects to the social and political world in which Socrates lived, and the world of ancient Greece, so different to our own in many beguiling respects, is a backdrop without which we cannot appreciate his peculiar uniqueness. In particular, we must consider the society of 5th-century Greece and the city-state of Athens, where intense political, military and social conflicts were inextricably linked to an astonishing rise and fall of greatness. The changing cultural climate that accompanied this rise and fall help situate and explain both the originality and the fate of Socrates.

Citizen of Athens

Socrates was born into a culture that constitutes one of the most creative and dynamic periods in the history of civilisation. By the time of his birth, only nine years after the momentous and decisive defeat of an invading Persian army at the battle of Plataea, the Greek world, and Athens in particular, had developed a cultural richness and a political independence that we acclaim with the term 'classical'. Sophocles was in his mid-twenties, Euripides was a teenager and Aeschylus, when Socrates was a two-year-old, had produced the *Persians*, the earliest surviving Greek tragedy, reminding Athenians of their glorious role in the defeat of the Persians at the naval battle of Salamis, the year before the conclusive battle of Plataea. Like those of the post-Second World War generation who flowered as hippies in the 1960s, Socrates was a child of his times, naively confident and bearing the aspirations of those who had paid the price for their freedom.

This Greek world invented democracy and argued about issues such as the nature of law and power, issues that remain at the heart of our sense of what it means to be a citizen living in a society that aspires to be just. The Greeks devised written forms of artistic expression – epic, lyric poetry, tragedy and comedy – and visual forms of art such as sculpture and architecture that continue to inspire, astonish and influence new generations of artists. In prose they explored history and philosophy in ways previously unknown.

Who were the people that did this, where did they come from and what made their achievements possible?

The obscure but important ancestors of Socrates and his fellow 5th-century Greeks were Indo-European tribes who spread outwards from somewhere in the vicinity of the Caucasus. Around 2000, when northern Europe was still in the Neolithic age, a branch of these people moved south into Greece and developed forms of living that drew upon those already existing in Greece as well as, crucially, other non-Greek cultures: the non-Indo-European Minoans of Crete, the Hittites who dominated central Anatolia, the older Near East world of Egypt, the Phoenicians at the eastern end of the Mediterranean, and the earliest civilization of all, that of Mesopotamia. In Greece itself there emerged the Bronze Age culture of the Mycenaeans – a world evoked in Homer's *Odyssey* and *Iliad* – which flourished until the downfall of their palace citadels around 1150. A so-called Dark Age followed, but the light of Europe's first civilization had not been extinguished and it re-emerged in the 8th century. The earliest surviving inscription in the language we call ancient Greek appears around 750 on a jug, 26 years after the first Olympic Games, and to a period not long after this time belongs the figure known as Homer.

'Atossa: But tell me: where, by men's reports, is Athens built?

Chorus: Far westward, where the sun-god sinks his fainting fires ...

Atossa: And are they skilled in archery?

Chorus: No, not at all: They carry stout shields, and fight hand-to-hand with spears.

Atossa: Who shepherds them? What master do their ranks obey?

Chorus: Master? They are not called servants to any man.

Atossa: And can they, masterless, resist invasion?'

Atossa, the mother of Xerxes who led the Persian invasion of Greece in 480, enquiring about Athens in Aeschlyus' *Persians*.[19]

A population increase, combined with a scarcity of farming land and the establishment of trade links, led to a great age of Greek colonisation that began in the mid-700s. By the time of Socrates, a Greek-speaking world lay scattered around the Mediterranean in at least a thousand different communities, from southern Spain to the Black Sea and southern Russia, including southern Italy, north Africa and the west coast of Turkey. In the Peloponnese of mainland Greece, Sparta was the largest community, covering some 8,000 square kilometres, three times the size of Athens.

The sense of a shared Greek identity was based around a common language and religion and the institution of the city-state (*polis*) that provided the foundation of community life. The city itself, with an open meeting and market area (*agora*) and seat of government, was only the focal point of the community's life; the area that each city-state laid claim to usually consisted of farm dwellings and villages that extended well beyond the city's confines. In the case of Athens, the chief city was the nucleus of the territory of Attica, about 2,500 square kilometres in extent. Whatever its size, a city-state was sufficiently free of external authority to inculcate a keen sense of autonomy amongst its members, even though it might sometimes be forced into alliances or dominated by stronger powers. In the 5th century, Sparta and Athens established domains and strongly enforced their rule, but the states under their control still governed their own domestic affairs. Moreover, there were no non-Greek powers involved: the autonomy of city-states was only curtailed by other Greek city-states. This was a proud claim by Greeks. There were, however, a variety of political structures. Oligarchies were common and took various forms, incorporating in Sparta a dual monarchy, while developments in Athens led by the middle of the 5th century to the less common system of democracy.

The various city-states all saw themselves as Greek, but this did not prevent rivalries and conflicts leading to war. An Athenian citizen like Socrates was part of a society that could never take peace for granted. Athens was at war, on average, for three out of

An engraving of Solon explaining his code of law to the Athenians

every four years throughout the 5th and 4th centuries, and when not fighting an external enemy the city experienced internal class conflicts that could, and did, lead to violence. The class war eventually led to a form of democracy that characterised the political culture that Socrates was born into. It originated in the early 6th century when Solon, an Athenian statesman who introduced a new code of law, established the right of the poorer class – or rather those of that class who were neither women, slaves nor non-Athenian residents – to attend the Assembly. The wealthy retained executive power but the practice of enslavement for debt was abolished.

After Solon, there followed a period of rule by tyrants, but in 510 the last tyrant was driven out of the city, paving the way for further political reforms by Cleisthenes around 508. Cleisthenes divided the Athenian people into ten newly-created tribes that cut across traditional lines of blood, basing them instead on the local village communities (*demes*) that made up the city-state. He also created a Council of 500 citizens, chosen annually by lot from the ten tribes, with each tribe taking its turn to serve as the 'Prytaneis' for 36 days in the Council year. The Prytaneis was a standing committee of the Council in permanent session, living in Council buildings during its term of office. The Council itself acted like a civil service, preparing the agenda for the Assembly. Over the next 40 years, further democratic reforms were introduced. The Areopagos, the old aristocratic council, was stripped of its powers and the rich lost their final bastion of political power. The Assembly and Council became the chief powers of the state. Regardless of social class, every adult male who was not a slave or a foreigner had the right to vote at the Assembly and each year a percentage of them were chosen by lot as jurors for the lawcourts. Small payments were introduced for attending the Assembly and the lawcourts, making it easier

'There had been tension and enmity for a long time between the nobles and the common people ... the nobles possessed all the land and if the poor failed to pay a rent they could be sold into slavery ... and so the many finally rose up against the few. And when the *stasis* (civil war) had become violent, both sides, in agreement, chose Solon to mediate between them.'

Aristotle, *Constitution of Athens*.[20]

for the poor to participate. Athens was very proud of its unusual democratic structures, something that emerges in contemporary sources, such as Thucydides the historian and the playwright Euripides, who wrote in *The Suppliants*: 'This city is free. It is not ruled by one man, but by all the people. Each year different people take political office, and the rich have no advantage, for even the poorest have equal rights.'[21]

The important exceptions to the random selection of government officials by lot were the ten generals who were elected into office on an annual basis. Athenians were not going to entrust their city's survival in war to a lottery and any general could be re-elected year after year if their continued service was deemed desirable. This was how Pericles achieved a pre-eminent position in Athenian politics for a period of three decades. Generals like Pericles stood accountable to the Assembly and there were formal occasions during their year of service when they could face complaints of poor conduct and, if necessary, be put on trial and punished.

Socrates, then, was born into a highly political culture, although the ancient Greeks' understanding of politics was different in many ways to our own. Key terms from our political vocabulary, like democracy and the word politics itself, have origins in ancient Greece; yet their modern meanings and connotations are generally very different from the ones taken for granted in 5th-century Athens. Our form of representative democracy involves voting once every few years for professional politicians who belong to highly organised and structured parties. Once in power, the politicians go about their business and most citizens are content to observe what they do from a distance, a process mediated by the mass media. Politics for Athenians was experienced in a far more direct way; a contemporary analogy might be made with atypical, politically intense communities like those of Derry or Belfast in the 1970s and 1980s. For Athenians, there was government but no Government: democracy was participatory and politics was the air they breathed – despite, or due to, the absence of professional politicians, parties and a mass media. In the first book of his *Politics*, Aristotle, writing in the late 4th century, famously identified man as 'a political animal' because he lived in a *polis*, and our word 'idiot' derives from the Greek for 'a private person', one who neglects his civic responsibilities. The Athenian Pericles echoed these sentiments in the 5th century, associating them with the nature of the city's democracy. 'Our constitution is called a democracy because power is in the hands not of a minority but of the whole people ... we do not say that a man who takes no interest in politics is a man who minds his own business; we say that he has no business here at all.'[22]

Rather than risk getting too dewy-eyed about the authenticity of Athens' participatory democracy, it is worth recalling that the citizen body was made up of only about 50,000 from a total population of around 350,000 in the middle of the 5th century. As well as a large slave population, perhaps as many as 100,000, all women and non-Athenian residents of the city were denied political rights. Moreover, the Assembly's meeting place could only hold about 6,000 people, one-eighth of the total citizenship, so the entire citizen body did not come together at Assembly meetings. Nevertheless, when all the forms of political participation are taken into account, including the law courts and a comprehensive system of local government that also involved all citizens, it seems fair to say that Athens achieved a remarkable level of democracy.

Without eulogizing Athenian democracy, it remains true that the negative, alienating connotations of the term 'politics' for a modern Western electorate are broadly absent from ancient Greek thought, perhaps because of a different perception of the relationship between state and individual. In a city-state, the individual's sense of being was so bound up with the community that there was little sense of individual rights that could conflict with those of the state. Greeks had one word for city, *astu,* referring to the urban space, and another word, *polis*, for the community of persons into which an individual was born. The city had an economic identity but the *polis* had its origins in a sense of tribal identity based on kinship, and even under the radical democracy that was taking shape in Athens as Socrates was growing up, citizenship was restricted to those whose father and mother were Athenian citizens. The origins of the *polis* help explain the ancient Greek understanding that the community comes before the individual. Socrates accepted this, though he stretched such an understanding to its limits.

Socrates was born in Athens in 470 or 469, in the deme of Alopeke, the son of Sophroniscus and Phaenarete. There was no registration of births in ancient Greece but it is known that his trial and condemnation took place in 399 and Plato has him state his age at that time to be 70: *this is my first appearance in a lawcourt, at the age of seventy.*[23]

Socrates' father is said to have been a skilled artisan, a stone-mason. Although this is never mentioned by Plato or Xenophon, it would be consistent with Socrates mentioning the mythical Daedalus as his ancestor, it being customary in ancient Greece for practitioners of a skill, traditionally passed down from father to son, to trace their lineage back to a mythical source.[24] Plato, who implies that Socrates' father was a respected member of his community who took care to see that his son was properly educated 'in the arts and in physical culture', makes no mention of him being a worker in stone.[25] Socrates' mother, Phaenarete, whose name means 'bringing virtue (*arete*) to light', was a midwife, her name and her work a wonderfully apt legacy to her son. Socrates himself used his mother's midwifery to illustrate the nature of his philosophy: *The difference is that I attend men and not women, and that I watch over the labour of their souls, not of their bodies.*[26]

Socrates was married to Xanthippe and they had three sons, of whom Lamprocles was the oldest, though under the age of 20 at the time of his father's execution. If Socrates was 70 when he died, this suggests he married late in life. Nothing is known for sure about Xanthippe and there is little firm basis for her reputation as a shrew. In the *Phaedo*, the only place in Plato where she is mentioned, Xanthippe comes across as a caring wife who attends him in prison. Xenophon's *Banquet* includes a passage which may be the source for the scurrilous stories that later developed about her character. Socrates is attending a formal drinking party, a symposium, and admiring the skill of the dancing girls. When he observes that women are not really inferior to men and that they are capable of learning anything, he is asked why then he does not teach Xanthippe to be more submissive, because she is 'beyond dispute, the most insupportable woman that is, has been, or ever will be'. The tone of the conversation is light and facetious and Socrates replies in the same mood, saying that just as a trainer of horses learns most when practising on a spirited animal, so he learned how to deal with all sorts of people by becoming accustomed to the temper of Xanthippe.[27] There is, however, also a passage in Xenophon where Lamprocles is angry with his mother and Socrates admonishes him for his ingratitude: *But what harm hath she done you? Hath she kicked you, or bit you, as wild beasts do when they are angry?* 'No', replies the son, 'but she utters such things as no one can bear from anybody.' *And you, Lamprocles, what have you not made this mother bear, with your continual cries and untoward restlessness! What fatigue in the day! What disturbance in the night! And what pangs when sickness at any time seized you!*[28]

Daedalus, inventor of mechanical devices, created the labyrinth for the Minotaur of Crete and later became the world's first aviator, escaping from the island with his son Icarus by constructing artificial wings. As a legendary craftsman and artist, Daedalus was credited with inventing various skills and tools essential to the stonemason's art.

A statue of Xanthippe from the Capitoline Museum, Rome

Later ancient writers, ignoring Socrates' defence of his wife and her caring image in Plato, amplified the suggestion that Xanthippe was feisty. This was sufficiently endorsed by Plutarch, writing some five centuries later, as to become an established legend by the time of Shakespeare, with Fielding referring to it in *Tom Jones*, and James Joyce having a character in *Ulysses* argue that Socrates learnt the art of dialectics from living with such an argumentative woman.[29] Even more shaky than the grounds for believing that Xanthippe was a shrew are those for bringing a second woman, Myrto, into Socrates' life, variously introduced as his first wife, his mistress or his second wife.[30] Neither Plato nor Xenophon refer to a second wife and when later writers do refer to Myrto it seems clear that truth is at a premium. Diogenes Laertius, for example, refers to other writers who report that Socrates took a second wife because of an Athenian law – for which there is not a shred of evidence – that sought to remedy the city's loss of its citizen population, due to the Peloponnesian War, by legitimising the children of men's extra-marital affairs.[31]

'He once said to Xanthippe, who first abused him, and then threw water at him, *Did I not say that Xanthippe was thundering now, and would soon rain?* ... Once she attacked him in the marketplace, and tore his cloak off ... And he used to say that one ought to live with a restive woman, just as horsemen manage violent-tempered horses.'

Diogenes Laertius, writing around the early 3rd century AD.[32]

It is likely that the young Socrates would have followed his father's trade, if indeed his father was ever a stonemason. Both Pausanias, the first travel writer, writing in the 2nd century AD, and Diogenes Laertius, early in the 3rd century AD, refer to a story that statues of the Graces on the Acropolis were the work of Socrates, but this seems to be a confusion with another Socrates (the name was not uncommon) because of the likely date of the sculptures.[33] What is more certain is that at some stage Socrates abandoned the kind of life he was expected to lead. He must have had some source of income to sustain his everyday living, though what exactly this was is not known. Plato emphasises that he did not teach in return for money and much later sources suggest that he was able to live off a modest investment accruing from his father.

The Socrates who emerged as a recognisable figure on the streets of Athens was not known as a craftsman but as an intellectual, popularly associated with a number of highbrow thinkers who visited the city and helped make Athens the intellectual capital of the Greek world. Ancient Greek philosophy originated around the beginning of the 6th century, in the Greek-colonised city-states of Ionia, on the west coast of modern Turkey. There, thinkers had first applied the exercise of reason to questions about the nature of reality. Individuals like Thales, Anaximander and Anaximenes had speculated about the underlying nature of the physical world and looked for a cosmic, elemental unity without recourse to myth and divine intervention. In the early 5th century, another Ionian, Heraclitus, saw a profound and dialectical order at work in the continuous process of change that made up the plurality of the world. Other philosophers hailed from Greek colonies in southern Italy and Sicily, to which the Ionian revolution had spread. Parmenides was one of these and he may have visited Athens and conversed with the young Socrates.

In the 5th century the centre of learning in the ancient world shifted from the city-states of the Greek colonies to Athens, whose patron goddess Athena was appropriately associated with wisdom. Her city became rich and famous and its blossoming democracy engendered a spirit of free speech and open debate that attracted philosophers from all parts of the Greek world. Socrates as a young man was living in interesting times and his intellect fed off these early philosophers: *When I was a young man I was wonderfully keen on that wisdom they call natural sciences, for I thought it splendid to know the causes of everything, why it comes to be, why it perishes and why it exists.*[34]

In 447, very soon after Athens formally established peace with Persia and around the same time that Parmenides is said to have visited Athens, a grand rebuilding programme got underway. The temples on the city's acropolis that had been destroyed in the Persian invasion of 480–479 were rebuilt and replaced by the iconic buildings that still stand there: the Parthenon, Propylaea, Erechtheum and Temple of Nike. The rebuilding programme included the renovation of the city's agora, also devastated by the Persians. The agora remained the civic heart of the city and its grand size, about 550 by 685 metres, allowed for large informal gatherings. It is here that Socrates is traditionally imagined engaging in his philosophical mission with fellow-citizens. A new painted colonnade, the Stoa Poikile, was constructed around it, and to one side a temple to Hephaestus was built. Crossing the agora was the street along which the four-yearly procession of the Great Panathenaia festival made its way up to the Parthenon.

'The greatness of our city brings it about that all the good things from all over the world flow in to us ... Our city is open to the world ... Future ages will wonder at us, as the present age wonders at us now.'

Pericles' funeral speech from Thucydides, *The Peloponnesian War.*[35]

Socrates was in his early twenties when building work on the Parthenon commenced and in his mid-thirties when it was completed in 432. These were golden years for Athens and there is reason for thinking that Socrates shared the pride and self-confidence in the city that Pericles expressed in 430 in his funeral oration for the citizens who had died in the first year of the Peloponnesian War. Years later, as part of his explanation for why he will not try to escape while awaiting execution, Socrates speaks of a moral contract he has made with Athens. He was always free to leave the city if there were aspects of Athenian life that he found intolerable. Socrates imagines the Laws of Athens addressing him: *You would not have dwelt here most consistently of all the Athenians if the city had not been exceedingly pleasing to you. You have never left the city, even to see a festival, nor for any other reason except military service; you have never gone to stay in any other city, as people do.*[36]

As is always the case with the early history of his life, nothing is known for sure, but a picture emerges of Socrates enjoying the cultural climate of Athens, his curiosity aroused by the early philosophers and their theories of natural causes. According to Theo-

A view of the Acropolis in the time of Socrates

phrastus, a 4th-century Greek philosopher, Socrates joined the school of Archelaus, an Athenian who had been a student of Anaxagoras, and this is confirmed by another writer, Aristoxenus.[37] At some stage, likely to have before his mid-thirties, Socrates found his faith in science to have been misplaced because the explanations on offer did not go to the heart of the matter: they explained how things worked but not why. In Plato's *Phaedo*, Socrates introduces an analogy for his change of direction. Just as those who watch an eclipse of the sun risk damaging their eyes, *I feared that my soul would be altogether blinded if I looked at things with my eyes and tried to grasp them with each of my senses. So I thought I must take refuge in discussions and investigate the truth of things by means of words.*[38] Xenophon also marks Socrates' divergence from the philosophers of nature – 'He demonstrated the folly of those who busied themselves much in such fruitless disquisitions, asking whether they thought they were already sufficiently instructed in human affairs, that they undertook only to meditate on divine?'[39] – while also recognising his acquaintance with such knowledge.[40]

Socrates began to devote himself to philosophy. The traditional belief that he lived in poverty points to a self-chosen act later in his life and not to his family background. The best evidence for this comes from the fact that, when he was past his mid-thirties, Socrates was serving in the Athenian infantry as a hoplite (an infantryman) at the start of the Peloponnesian War against Sparta (431–404). Athenian citizenship and the preparedness to fight for Athens went together naturally – it was never a question of being conscripted or volunteering – but the capacity in which a citizen fought was related to his social class. The hoplites were a heavy infantry force, made up of citizens who were able to provide their own equipment and, as this was moderately expensive, only those within a certain property band were assigned to the hoplite ranks. About 30–40 per cent of citizens fell within this category, each owning on average around 7 acres of land.[41] Such citizens were expected to maintain in serviceable condition a shield (*hoplon*), a bronze helmet, a two-piece bronze breastplate and a 2–3-metre wooden spear tipped with iron.

Hostilities between Sparta and Athens had been brewing for many years, fuelled by Athenian imperial ambitions and the suspicion and envy this engendered in Sparta, traditionally the most militarised of the Greek city-states. The superior quality of the Spartan hoplite forces had been largely responsible for turning back, against all the odds, the invasion of the Greek mainland by the mighty Persian empire at the battle of Plataea in 479. Athens, whose military power lay in her navy, had contributed to the defeat of the Persians and chose to capitalize on her victory by forming an alliance with other Greek states. What was initially a defensive alliance, in the face of a continuing threat from Persia, evolved into an Athenian empire that came to control most of the Greek states in and around the Aegean Sea. Each member state of the defensive alliance made financial contributions and the funds were stored on the island of Delos, hence the name Delian League, given to the alliance by modern historians. As the Persian threat diminished, doubts about the nature and purpose of the Delian League increased. In 454 the funds on Delos were transferred to Athens and from then on it was clear that the Athenians would dictate the League's affairs. The wealth created by the empire poured into Athens and helped make the city the cultural centre of the Greek world.

The Athenian empire included a state in the northwest of the Aegean, Potidaea, which had close links with Corinth, a traditional enemy of Athens and an ally of Sparta. Athens put pressure on Potidaea to sever its links with Corinth, while Corinth and others encouraged the city-state to revolt against Athens. Supported by a promise of support from Sparta, Potidaea duly declared her independence from Athens in the spring of 432 and the revolt spread to neighbouring city-states. A Corinthian force was dispatched to help defend Potidaea and Athens responded by sending its own troops. The Athenian force defeated the Corinthians and proceeded to lay siege to Potidaea. These events were the opening salvos in what became the Peloponnesian War after Athens formally rejected a set of demands from Sparta in 431, including one that the siege of Potidaea be lifted.

Athenian forces besieged Potidaea for 30 months before the city finally surrendered in the winter of 430/29. It was this long campaign that saw Socrates in active service on behalf of Athens. It is not known how long he was there, but he could have arrived with the first Athenian force in the winter of 433/2. In Plato's *Symposium,* his friend Alcibiades, who was stationed alongside Socrates, marvelled at his ability to endure the harsh winters: '[He] went out in that weather wearing nothing but this same old light cloak, and even

'The following terms were agreed upon: the Potidaeans, with their wives and children and auxiliary forces, were to be permitted to leave the town, the men to be allowed to take one garment apiece, the women two; they were also allowed to take with them a fixed sum of money for their journey.'

Thucydides, *The Peloponnesian War.*[42]

in bare feet he made better progress on the ice than the other soldiers did in their boots.' He adds a detail that suggests how Socrates could unintentionally irritate others: 'You should have seen the looks they gave him; they thought he was only doing it to spite them.'[43] It was while stationed at Potidaea that Alcibiades noticed another instance of Socrates' powers of endurance, the incident already referred to where he stood alone all night in a trance-like state of meditation, striking those who did not know him as a very strange individual. Nevertheless, his fellow soldiers would doubtless have appreciated Socrates' personal loyalty when he saved Alcibiades' life during a battle at Potidaea: 'he just refused to leave me behind when I was wounded, and he rescued not only me but my armour as well.'[44]

The Potidaea campaign was not the only episode of military service for Socrates. Eight years later, when he was in his mid-forties, he took part in the battle of Delium, evidence not only of his physical fitness but also of Athens' growing need for able soldiers in the face of increasing losses in the ongoing Peloponnesian War. The number of citizens had been reduced by losses on battlefields and by a deadly plague which struck the city at the end of the first year of the war and claimed a quarter or perhaps a third of the population. The plague was also carried by reinforcements sent to Potidaea when the siege was in its 25th month, and 1,500 hoplites died from it in the camp. Thucydides, the Athenian historian who chronicled the war and survived catching the plague himself, gives a harrowing description of the course of the epidemic. He witnessed the physical and moral effects, drawing attention to the ways in which the calamity undermined people's faith in religion and civilized values. 'As for what is called honour, no one showed himself willing to abide by its laws, so doubtful was it whether one would survive to enjoy the name for it ... As for the gods, it seemed to be the same thing whether one worshipped them or not, when one saw the good and the bad dying indiscriminately. As for

The battle of Potidaea. At the centre of the conflict Socrates saves the life of Alcibiades. After a drawing by Carstens

offences against human law, no one expected to live long enough to be brought to trial and punished.'[45]

In the summer of 429, the third year of the war, Pericles, the Athenian statesman who had championed democracy and led his city-state into the war against Sparta, caught the plague and died. His two sons had also fallen victim, leaving him without an heir, and the Assembly passed a special decree legitimizing his natural son through his mistress Aspasia. The death of Pericles left the conduct of the war in the hands of lesser figures who in time would question the wisdom of the war policy he had implemented. Pericles' policy had always been to use the unrivalled strength of the Athenian navy, avoiding all action on land, where the superior forces of the Spartans were likely to prevail. He had successfully argued for the building of the Long Walls, two parallel walls about 200 metres apart, connecting Athens with the port of Piraeus so that provisions could reach the city directly by sea.

In 428 this policy still prevailed and proved highly effective in quashing rebellion on the Aegean island of Lesbos. A squadron of ships set sail to the island and blockaded the harbour of Mytilene, the most important town on Lesbos, while a larger squadron cruised the surrounding area, deterring Sparta from sending help. Mytilene surrendered the following year. What happened next, when compared to the aftermath of the fall of Potidaea only a few years earlier, illustrates the corrosive effect of the war on Athenian attitudes. The Assembly debated what was to be done over Mytilene. Cleon argued for a hard-line policy and won. The entire male population would be put to death, the women and children enslaved. The next day, however, the Assembly debated the subject again and a narrow majority rescinded the decision. Only those held responsible for the rebellion would die. Yet moral revulsion played no part here – only the practical argument that a policy of wholesale executions would not help in winning the war.

'If Cleon's method is adopted, can you not see that every city will not only make more careful preparations for revolt, but will also hold out against siege to the very end, since to surrender early or late means just the same thing? This is, unquestionably, against our interests.;

From the Assembly's debate over Mytilene.[46]

In the years after Mytilene there emerged a more reckless attitude to the conduct of the war, and in 425 this resulted in a notable victory for Athens. A Spartan force which had landed on the island of Sphacteria was blockaded by an Athenian fleet. In the Assembly, Cleon criticized the leading general in charge of the operation for taking too long to secure victory. Then it was suggested that Cleon himself, if he was so much wiser, should take charge of the operation and show how it should be done. Cleon did just that, landing a large force on the island, killing a third of the enemy and securing the surrender of 120 Spartan citizen-warriors. Traditionally, Spartans never surrendered. The shock induced

Sparta to sue for peace in return for the safe release of the prisoners. Cleon, now at the height of his influence, saw a chance to gain new territory and, departing radically from Pericles' policy, spurned the chance to make a peace that Sparta could accept. Instead, in 424, he initiated a large-scale invasion of Boeotia, a region to the north of Athens, but this time everything did not go according to plan. The Athenian land forces were engaged by the Boeotian army, and in the ensuing battle of Delium the Athenians were soundly defeated, losing over 1,000 hoplites.

One of the Greeks who survived the mauling at Delium was Socrates, and Alcibiades, who was also there though this time serving in the cavalry, witnessed his friend's coolness in the stressful context of a hasty withdrawal. Socrates, he recalls, always keeping a watchful eye on the situation and showing a grim determination not to be picked off by the enemy, not only saved himself with dignity and courage but also helped his fellow-hoplite, Laches, to survive the ordeal. In the *Laches*, Plato has Laches himself tell the story and conclude that 'if the rest had been willing to behave in the same manner, our city would be safe and we would not then have suffered a disaster of that kind'.[47]

Socrates refers to his military experience when on trial for his life and as well as citing Potidaea and Delium he also mentions service at Amphipolis. In August 424, before

'He was observing everything quite calmly, looking out for friendly troops and keeping an eye on the enemy. Even from a great distance it was obvious that this was a very brave man, who would put up a terrific fight if anyone approached him. This is what saved both of them. For, as a rule, you try to put as much distance as you can between yourself and such men in battle; you go after the others, those who run away helter-skelter.'

Alcibiades' account of Socrates at the battle of Delium.[48]

the battle of Delium took place, the Spartans had sent a small army into Chalcidice, the region in the northwest of the Aegean that included Potidaea, to stir up further dissent against Athens.

They hoped to capture the Athenian colony of Amphipolis and its strategic location on the road that led to the Hellespont and the Bosporus in the east, the route for ships carrying Athens' essential grain supply. The Spartans were under the leadership of one of their best generals, Brasidas, and they took Amphipolis in 424. Cleon, thinking he could repeat the kind of success he had achieved at Sphacteria, sailed from Athens in 422 with an army. In the battle, both Cleon and Brasidas were killed and Socrates, now aged 47, was again on the losing side. The battle was a disastrous defeat for Athens and it precipitated a temporary peace in the Peloponnesian War.[49] It was nearly ten years since the first invasion of Attica in 431 and Athenians were war-weary; Aristophanes' *Peace*, produced in the spring of 421, just before peace terms were agreed, gave expression to the longing for an end to the war.

'And call to mind, my comrades
The good old days we lived in
That once were ours in peacetime:
Dried fruits and figs and myrtles,
The bounties of the harvest,
The vintages, the violets
In clusters by the fountain,
The ever-welcome olives –'

From Aristophanes' *Peace*.[50]

Socrates' military record, then, is an impressive one; but while he comes across as physically quite a remarkable individual, he was a long way from resembling the handsome male citizen of the type idealised in Greek art of this period. Aristophanes' *Clouds* was produced on the stage one year after the battle of Delium, and his portrayal of Socrates' appearance, which presumably was one that the audience could be expected to recognise, is not a flattering one. His poor taste in dress and characteristic state of shoelessness becomes material for Aristophanes' humour; and this may be related to Plato's story of Socrates going barefoot and wearing light clothing in winter.[51] In Plato's *Symposium*, Alcibiades compares him to a satyr: 'Now look at him again! Isn't he also just like the satyr Marsyas. Nobody, not even you, Socrates, can deny

A sympathetic drawing of Socrates by Perugino in the Uffizi Gallery, Florence

that you *look* like them. But the resemblance goes beyond appearance, as you're about to hear.'[52] Satyrs were portrayed as grotesque goat-like creatures or humans with horses' tails and ears, so Alcibiades is hardly suggesting that Socrates had a fetching figure. In Aristophanes' comedy, there is a remark about the philosopher's darting eyes that seems designed to raise a laugh, and Xenophon relates a conversation where Socrates himself playfully makes use of this idiosyncrasy of his to score a point in a most judicious manner. With his tongue firmly in his cheek, Socrates employs his characteristic method of philosophical argument, looking at everyday examples of the issue under discussion and drawing logical conclusions. He agrees with a handsome young man called Critobulus that beauty is to be found in both the animal and the human worlds. Socrates wonders how forms so different could share such a common quality. Critobulus feels sure he know why this could be the case:

'Critobulus: Because they are well made, either by art or nature, for the purposes they are employed in.

Socrates: Do you know the use of eyes?

Critobulus: To see.

Socrates: Well! it is for that very reason mine are handsomer than yours.

Critobulus: Your reason?

Socrates: Yours see only in a direct line; but, as for mine, I can look not only directly forward, as you, but sideways too, they being seated on a kind of ridge on my face, and staring out.

Critobulus: At that rate a crab has the advantage of all other animals in matter of eyes?

Socrates: Certainly.'[53]

In a similar vein, Socrates goes on to demonstrate that he possesses a more handsome nose than Critobulus because, compared to his normal, downward-facing nose, Socrates has a wide one that is turned upwards and therefore capable of retrieving smells from

A finely detailed bust of Socrates

many directions. To cap it all, Socrates can ask, *Don't you believe too that my kisses are more luscious and sweet than yours, having my lips so thick and large?*[54] Nietzsche, recalling this passage from Xenophon, describes a Socrates with 'crab-like eyes' and 'puffed-up lips' as 'the first great Hellene to be ugly'.[55]

Socrates' witty remark about the superior quality of his kisses introduces another aspect of his life as an Athenian citizen, his sexuality. There is no ancient Greek word that corresponds to our term 'homosexual' because the question of whether one's sexual partner was of the same or the opposite sex was not what chiefly mattered in that society. The appropriateness or otherwise of particular sexual relations was governed by social norms concerning the age, social standing and gender of the participants. Any male in a superior role, defined by age, gender or status, could regard sexual relations with their inferior as normal, whether that person was of the same or different sex. This generalisation, however, risks simplifying an area of ancient Greek life which was complex and nuanced in various ways. In Athenian society, and probably in the Greek world more generally, homoerotic relationships between boys (aged between puberty and the growth of a beard) and older men were considered quite normal. At the same time, a need was felt to safeguard the social reputation of adolescent Athenian males: licentious sexual behaviour was considered shameful. A boy could be courted by an older man and a homoerotic relationship, which we would call homosexual, willingly consummated, but sexual etiquette ensured that the boy's role remained passive.

Socrates was no different to other Athenians of his class in being attracted to young men, as Plato makes clear in *Charmides*. Renowned for his good looks and sexual appeal, the young Charmides stirs Socrates' interest when he sees him for the first time since he was a child. *That men of my age should have been affected this way was natural enough*, he says, but when Charmides sits down next to him he is even more physically aroused: *I saw inside his cloak and caught on fire and was quite beside myself.*[56] There is an anecdote in Plato's *Symposium* that is also testimony to the naturalness with which homosexual relations between a young person and an older man were regarded by 5th-century Athenians of the class that Socrates was mixing with. Alcibiades relates how, as a young man just under 20 years old, he was happy at the thought of being courted by Socrates and engineered a situation where they would be alone together. When this led nowhere, Alcibiades decided to reverse the normal roles of such a situation and take the initiative by inviting Socrates to dinner and keeping him so late that it would be natural for him to stay the night. 'The lights were out; the slaves had left; the time was right, I thought, to come to the point and tell him freely what I had in mind.'[57] Alcibiades offers himself to Socrates, saying how he would feel honoured by a sexual relationship with a wise philosopher. 'I slipped underneath the cloak and put my arms around this man ... he turned me down! He spurned my beauty, of which I was so proud ... be sure of it, I swear to you by all the gods and goddesses together, my night with Socrates went no further than if I had spent it with my own father or older brother.'[58]

Alcibiades dates this failure of his to before the battle of Potidaea, when Socrates was in his late thirties, and he tells the story to show the kind of qualities that he so admired in the older man. He respects his fortitude, self-control and moderation and goes on to give other examples that arose in the course of their military service together. Alcibiades marvels at Socrates' ability to withstand hunger and his moderation in drinking, adding though that when he did find himself part of a heavy drinking bout 'he could drink the best of us under the table. Still, and most amazingly, no one ever saw him drunk.'[59] This is the context in which Alcibiades relates the stories of Socrates' trance-like state that lasted for most of a day and all through the night, his bravery during the battle of Potidaea and his coolness under fire during the retreat from Delium. As if to prove the truth of what he was saying, the symposium is then interrupted by the arrival of a group of drunken revellers and another drinking session gets underway. They all continue talking through the night, some eventually leaving for home and others falling asleep where they sat. By dawn the next morning only two are still awake and able to listen to Socrates discussing why a good dramatist should be able to write both comedies and tragedies. First one of them, the playwright Aristophanes, who lampooned Socrates in his *Clouds*, falls asleep and then the other does as well. All this is observed by one of the party who had fallen asleep earlier and woken up at dawn to see Socrates getting up to leave. Plato records how 'He said that Socrates went directly to the Lyceum, washed up, spent the rest of the day just as he always did, and only then, as evening was falling, went home to rest.'[60]

All the little that is known about the life of Socrates up to his mid-forties, around the year 422, makes it difficult to understand why someone like this could be deemed an enemy of the state and put on trial for his life. His war record is exemplary and in many respects he exhibits qualities that make him a model Greek citizen. He is dutiful, courageous, conscientious and law-abiding, known for his ability to endure physical hardships, hold his drink and practise self-control. At the same time, though, Socrates is different to the average Athenian citizen. He is an intellectual with no proper occupation, eccentric in his tendency to lose himself in thought for hours, becoming oblivious to others, careless in his dress and humorously indifferent to his own ugliness. In middle age, Socrates must have been a sufficiently well-known character on the streets of Athens for his eccentricity to be lampooned by Aristophanes in his comedy *Clouds*. There is also the hint of a dark note in his characterisation in Aristophanes, where he is associated with a type of professional intellectual who makes a living by teaching dubious rhetorical skills. He is also associated in *Clouds* with philosophers of natural science whose theories could be caricatured as atheistic and inimical to right-thinking citizens. On the one hand, Socrates was part of an intellectual enlightenment that helped make Athens a renowned city of the arts and its citizens proud of their cultural and political achievements, but on the other, here was a very odd middle-aged man, someone who preferred to discuss and argue about ideas instead of getting on with a normal job like the majority of Athenians. He was probably disliked, even feared, by traditionalists.

In his mid-forties, then, Socrates was a well-known individual, eccentric in his ways, probably disliked by some but with good friends who respected him highly. Some 25 years passed before he was put on trial and it is these years that hold the key to understanding why some people felt such an unconventional intellectual had to be silenced. The two decades were years of war and struggle for Athens – the glorious period that Pericles rhapsodically described in his funeral speech was becoming a nostalgic memory – and bitter political struggles were dividing Athenians against themselves. The traumatised and insecure Athenian society that put Socrates on trial in 399 was very different to the ebullient world that he had been born into 70 years earlier.

It is the year 406 before anything more is known about the life of Socrates. By then the Peloponnesian War had long since resumed – the peace treaty of 421 had barely lasted three years – and although Athens had won some victories, there had also been defeats and the strains of a long war were making themselves felt. When Athenian ships were blockaded by a Spartan fleet in Lesbos in the eastern Aegean, a decision was made hastily to assemble a new fleet and attempt a rescue. Such was the shortage of citizens able to crew the ships, the Assembly voted to use every man capable of service, including slaves and resident foreigners. The upper age limit for military service was 50 and although there was no question of enrolling Socrates, now in his early 60s, he did play a role in what happened after the sea battle of Arginusae in 406. During the battle, the inexperienced crews of Athenians rose to the occasion and destroyed 70 enemy ships at the cost of only 15 of their own. A dozen more Athenian ships suffered damage and lay waterlogged in the sea, their crews awaiting assistance. The Athenian generals pursued the remnants of the Spartan fleet, a storm developed, and in the following confusion the plight of the damaged ships was forgotten. They sank with the loss of all their crews.

Despite the triumphant victory, the generals were severely criticized for not rescuing the crews in the damaged ships. The mood in Athens turned ugly. It was proposed that all six of the generals who had returned to Athens should be tried and executed if convicted of gross negligence. Such a group trial was unconstitutional – under Athenian law each accused person had the right to a separate trial – and it was up to the executive Council of 500 to prevent such a motion being put to the Assembly. It so happened at the time that Socrates was among those chosen by lot to serve on the Council and he was also in the group holding the presidency (*prytaneia*) of the Council. Members of this group were bullied and threatened into allowing the illegal motion – but not Socrates. However, his protests were brushed aside and the motion to prosecute the generals as one group was put to the Assembly and passed. All six generals were executed, including the younger Pericles, son of Pericles and Aspasia.

This was illegal, as you all recognised later. I was the only member of the presiding committee to oppose your doing something contrary to the laws, and I voted against it. The orators were ready to prosecute me and take me away, and your shouts were egging them on, but I thought I should run any risk on the side of law and justice.[61]

Socrates defending his action after the battle of Arginusae.

Arginusae turned out to be the last Athenian victory in the Peloponnesian War. In the spring of 404, Athens offered unconditional surrender and the city-state's democracy was replaced by a pro-Spartan oligarchy. Such was the ruthless brutality of their regime, which lasted less than a year, that the oligarchs became known as the Thirty Tyrants. Democrats were seized and summarily executed; others fled and went into exile. For the second time in as many years, Socrates, now aged 65, found himself facing a difficult political decision. The oligarchs tried to implicate others in their junta and they ordered Socrates along with four others to go and arrest a democrat, Leon of Salamis. *When the oligarchy was established, the Thirty summoned me to the Hall, along with four others, and ordered us to bring Leon from Salamis, that he might be executed.*[62] Socrates refused their demand and went home, leaving the other four to obey the order. Very soon after, the Thirty Tyrants lost power following a violent counter-revolution in 403 and a democracy was restored. It was this democracy which three years later put Socrates on trial and sentenced him to death.

The outcome of the war and its radical consequences for the political and social climate of Athens were to affect Socrates in ways that he could not have foreseen. He found himself facing enmity in a vulnerable situation and without powerful friends. The consequences were to prove fatal.

Friends and Enemies

To appreciate how the political and social climate had changed by the time Socrates faced trial, it will be helpful to return to the history of the Peloponnesian War and see how some individuals who were known to Socrates behaved during its course.

Sometimes, as Socrates discovered, you can make enemies because of who your friends are. Some of the people who had been associated with Socrates in the past became political players during and immediately after the Peloponnesian War and, as a result of the political decisions and allegiances they made, their reputations were sullied. They earned an opprobrium that could do little but harm to someone who was thought to have influenced them. One of these political players was Alcibiades, the character who turns up at the drinking party described in Plato's *Symposium*, praising Socrates for his military valour and revealing in his rueful confession the qualities of self-control and fortitude shown by Socrates when the young and adoring Alcibiades offered his body to him. Being associated with the glamorous but notorious Alcibiades, someone whose moral values proved to be spectacularly shaky, could only work against Socrates' best interests in the embittered body politic that took shape after the Peloponnesian War.

Alcibiades rose to political and military prominence during a heady and reckless period in the war. The defeat of Athens at Amphipolis, where Socrates saw active service for the last time, had led to a truce with Sparta. It was known as the Peace of

Nicias, after the Athenian general who brought it about in 421, but it could not contain the volatile rivalries between the Greek city states during this period. Corinth, Argos, Thebes and Sicily were all involved in political and military conflicts that strained the formal but uneasy peace between Athens and Sparta. Alcibiades was elected a general in 420 when he reached 30, the minimum age for the office, and he pursued a more aggressive policy than Nicias. Hostilities took on a vicious complexion when the island of Melos refused to aid Athens in 416 and a blockade by sea and land was set up by Athens. It was a bullying strategy; and when the island surrendered, a bloodthirsty punishment was inflicted on the inhabitants. Thucydides wrote a terse statement of what happened and in his very next sentence introduced the decision by Athens to invade the far larger island of Sicily, noting snappishly the lack of forethought that characterised the decision.

'The Melians surrendered unconditionally to the Athenians, who put to death all the men of military age whom they took, and sold the women and children as slaves. Melos itself they took over for themselves, sending out later a colony of 500 men.

In the same winter the Athenians resolved to sail against Sicily ... They were for the most part ignorant of the size of the island and of the numbers of its inhabitants, both Hellenic and native, and they did not realise that they were taking on a war of almost the same magnitude as their war against the Peloponnesians.'

Thucydides, *The Peloponnesian War*.[63]

Alcibiades was re-elected general in 415 and he strongly supported the plan to invade Sicily. Along with Nicias, who had argued against the invasion, he was appointed in joint command of the expedition, but soon after arriving was recalled to Athens to answer a charge of impiety arising from the mutilation of stone herms at Athens. The herms had been vandalized under cover of darkness, just before the fleet set sail, and when Athenians awoke on the morning of 7 June 415 to discover the outrage, some suspected an organised plot, all but one of the numerous herms

The ruins of the Arch of Adrian inside the Sanctuary of Eleusis

having been mutilated. A political motive seemed possible, for as Hermes was the god of travellers, the sacrilege could be seen as the work of a group opposed to the invasion force setting sail for Sicily.

The Assembly ordered an inquiry and, although the culprits were not to be found, the investigation uncovered other irreverent acts. Stories emerged about impious acts by inebriated young aristocrats parodying the sacred mysteries of Eleusis. Alcibiades was named as one of those involved; and malicious gossip spread by his political opponents suggested he was also behind the mutilation of the herms, though this was illogical given his enthusiasm for the Sicilian expedition. Alcibiades denounced his accusers and offered to stand trial but, according to Thucydides, his political enemies preferred to have him away in Sicily before they mounted a plot against him.

When Alcibiades was recalled, it was to answer charges relating to the profanation of the Eleusinian Mysteries, not the mutilation of the herms; but the atmosphere in Athens was so feverish that religious and political offences were conflated. A group of aristocratic young men were under suspicion, engendering fears of an oligarchic plot, and the law prohibiting the torture of citizens to obtain testimony was suspended in the general panic. It was not a good time for someone like Alcibiades to be facing the accusation of a religious offence and he chose to take flight and make his way to Sparta. This made him a traitor, especially after he gave advice to the Spartans about sending a contingent to Sicily to support the forces under siege there in Syracuse. In Athens he was condemned to death and the Eleusinian priests were called on to curse his name.

Meanwhile, the Sicilian expedition turned into a military disaster for Athens. Some 7,000 were taken prisoner and kept under such harsh conditions that most of them died. Plutarch relates the story of how some survived when the Syracusans discovered they could recite passages from the plays of Euripides.[64] When news of the defeat reached Athens in late 413 – a foreigner is said to have told a barber in Piraeus, who went straight to Athens with the news only to find no one would believe him – it was feared that the scale of the defeat could force Athens into surrendering to Sparta. The pressure on Athens mounted

Alcibiades, born 451/0, was the son of an Athenian general and was a child when his father died on the battlefield. The young Alcibiades was taken in by Pericles, both of them members of the noble and very influential Alcmaeonid family. Growing up in this illustrious family, Alcibiades acquired a reputation as a flamboyant young aristocrat with charisma, good looks and a clever mind. He became a friend of Socrates but with his political connections and ambitions he seemed fast-tracked for a dazzling public career. Like Socrates, he took part in the siege of Potidaea and fought in the battle of Delium. Typical of his ostentatious style and flair for publicity, he entered seven chariots for the Olympic Games of 416 and came away with first, second and fourth places.

when the Aegean island of Chios revolted in 412 and took the side of Sparta. The island of Samos became the chief naval base for Athenian attempts to contain both the threat of more rebellions and the new danger posed by Spartan overtures to Persia for aid in conclusively defeating her enemy.

Travellers and shepherds looked to Hermes, the herald of the gods, for good luck and protection. Safe routes were marked out in the form of stone pillars called 'herms'. These pillars carried a bust of Hermes and an erect phallus, symbol of masculine strength. They were placed along public routes as milestones and at the doorways of private homes, soliciting the guardianship of the god.

'This was the greatest Hellenic action that took place during this war, and in my opinion, the greatest action that we know of in Hellenic history – to the victors the most brilliant of successes, to the vanquished the most calamitous of defeats; for they were utterly and entirely defeated; their sufferings were on an enormous scale; their losses were, as they say, total; army, navy, everything was destroyed, and, out of many, only few returned. So ended the events in Sicily.'[65]

For the first 20 years of the Peloponnesian War, the democracy of Athens had held together with remarkable resilience. Following Pericles' advice, the people had gathered behind the Long Walls for safety and watched as Spartan armies invaded Attica each year and laid waste to their land and homes. The plague had wreaked havoc on an enclosed and confined community and now events in Sicily were experienced as a psychological and military disaster for which Thucydides could find no parallel. To some, Thucydides included, the debacle in Sicily could be traced back to the inherent vagaries of the democratic system and in 411 a group of Athenian aristocrats felt emboldened to intervene and establish an oligarchy. A Council of 400 was installed to rule Athens, a hundred years since the birth of democracy, when the last tyrant had been expelled from the city.

The oligarchs were challenged by the Athenian sailors based in Samos who, like the anarchist sailors at Kronstadt in Russia in 1921, saw themselves as defenders of a radical democracy. They wanted to sail to Athens to depose the Council of 400, but had to respond instead to revolts in the northern Aegean and to a menacing Spartan fleet in that region that endangered the Athenians' essential supply line for grain.

At this critical juncture, Alcibiades reappeared on the scene. After Sicily, he had continued to give advice to the Spartans, but they began to distrust him – in keeping with his scandalous reputation, it was said that when an earthquake drove people from their beds one night, he was seen emerging from the chamber of the Spartan king's wife – and after arriving in Asia Minor on behalf of Sparta, he changed sides once again. He negotiated unsuccessfully with the Persians to secure their support on the side of Athens but then the rebellious Athenian fleet at the Aegean island of Samos made him their general.

Eleusis, a deme of Athens, gave its name to a religious cult whose activities involved bathing in the sea, processions and the shouting of obscenities, culminating in a ritual at Eleusis where the secret proceedings were only known to initiates. The activities of this agrarian cult took place in September, at the time of sowing. The origins and meaning of the Eleusinian Mysteries relate to the myth of Demeter, the goddess of corn, and the abduction to the Underworld of her daughter Persephone for the months of winter, symbolizing the 'death' of plants between autumn and spring.

Back in Athens, splits deepened amongst the Council of 400 after some of them called upon the Spartans to enter the city. Civil strife erupted and the short-lived coup was deposed, with government entrusted to a restricted democracy of 5,000 before full democracy was restored in 410. In the Aegean, Alcibiades began conducting naval operations on the Athenian side and in 410 he won an outstanding naval victory at Cyzicus. This restored the safety of Athens' food supplies, damaged Spartan morale and helped keep the Peloponnesian War going for another six years. Alcibiades was cautious about returning to Athens and waited until 407 when he more felt confident about answering the religious charges still hanging over him. When he did return he was hailed as a hero by some and his confiscated property was restored, although it is not known if he and Socrates met up again. Perhaps Alcibiades was too busy, for he was once again appointed a general and then, in another twist of fortune, he was held responsible for the naval defeat at Notium in 406. Once more, he decided on a hasty retreat. He ended up at Gallipoli, where he was later murdered by unknown assailants, most likely the result of having accumulated one too many a political enemy over the course of his fickle life. Alcibiades' career was so extraordinarily turbulent and his personal and political life so full of scandals that Socrates' association with him – the older man in a position to influence the wayward young aristocrat – could only do the philosopher harm.

'Dionysus: ... what do you think
                    ... Of Alcibiades? ...
Euripides: What does the City think?
Dionysus: Loves, hates, wants to have him.
                    But what do *you* think? Tell us!
Euripides: I hate that citizen
                    Who is loath to serve his country,
                    Self-helpful and state-helpless.
Dionysus: Good, by Poseidon! Aeschylus,
                    What do you say?
Aeschylus: I say
                    It's best not to rear a lion
                    In the State – but if you do,
                    It's best to humour it...

(Aristophanes, *Frogs*, produced in 405, the year before the end
                                        of the Peloponnesian War.)[66]

It was not only Alcibiades who was known to have been a companion of the city's best-known intellectual. Socrates was also associated with Charmides, the very handsome young man by whom Socrates is aroused in Plato's eponymous dialogue. Charmides was an maternal uncle of Plato's and Critias, the other main character in *Charmides* and another associate of Socrates, was also related to Plato. The family to which they belonged was very wealthy and distinguished: its origins could be traced back to before Solon at the beginning of the 6th century. The aristocratic back-

'The *Paralus* [a fast messenger ship] arrived in Athens at night and announced the disaster, and a wailing came from the Piraeus, through the Long Walls, to the city, one man passing the word to another, so that on that night no one slept. They wept not only for the men who had been killed but even more for themselves.'

Xenophon describing news of Aegospotami reaching Athens.[67]

ground of this family helps explain the antidemocratic instincts of Charmides and Critias and, unlike Plato, who for the most part kept his politics within the safer confines of academic life, they chose to act on their political beliefs after the Peloponnesian War came to an end in 404.

The final battle in the war had taken place in 405, when the Athenian fleet was attacked by the Spartans under the command of Lysander at Aegospotami and surrendered in large numbers. Possibly as many as 4,000 seamen were captured and Lysander had them all massacred the following day, news of which terrified Athens when it reached the city. Athens was now without a fleet and thus cut off from supplies of corn, and her allies in Asia Minor were surrendering and handing over their Athenian garrisons to the Spartans. What followed was a blockade of the Piraeus, the port of Athens connected to the city by the defensive Long Walls, and although the inhabitants held out for as long as possible, starvation and riots made an unconditional surrender unavoidable.

Some of Athens' enemies, like Corinth and Thebes, wanted the defeated city destroyed altogether: Plutarch quotes a Corinthian proposal that the city be razed to the ground and the country-side left as pasture for herds of sheep. Sparta, which probably did not relish the prospect of either of these cities filling the power vacuum that a destroyed Athens would create, was content with seeing the Long Walls destroyed, the Athenian fleet restricted to twelve vessels and the democracy dismantled. The walls of Athens began to be pulled down on 4 March 404, according to an account by Xenophon, 'with much alacrity, music playing all the time'.[68] For the defeated Athenians, it was an ignominious conclusion to a war that had lasted 27 years and may have cost the lives of as many as one in every two citizens. A period of 76 years separated the defeat of the Persians at the battle of Salamis from the battle of Aegospotami; and in those seven decades, Athens had gone from a state of ebullient victory and cultural supremacy to one of lost empire, disillusionment, the defeat of democracy and naked, bloodthirsty political conflict.

The city-state that was forced to open its gates to Lysander and the triumphant Spartans was a broken and divided community. The war had exposed and exacerbated these divisions seven years earlier when the democracy was overthrown and the Council of 400 installed. In the counter-coup, some of the oligarchs had been tried and executed, but many had fled to Sparta. These men and their supporters now returned to Athens where, with the might of Sparta behind them, they forced the Assembly to create a committee of 30 citizens which would oversee the introduction of a new constitution.

Charmides was one of the Thirty, although it was Critias, the most prominent of the group, whose name became synonymous with the reign of terror that followed. Like a right-wing dic-tatorship in Latin America, with Sparta playing the role of the United States, the Thirty set about eliminating their political opponents. Democrats were arrested and executed, their property confiscated and used to bankroll the Spartan military. Supporters of the deposed democracy who escaped the knock on the door fled Athens, including one individual named Anytus, and anyone who remained in the city was subject to intimidation and the threat of arbitrary punishment.

Critias and Charmides, being former associates of Socrates, may have thought they could rely on his support when they ordered him to participate in the arrest of Leon of Salamis. In his trial, Socrates offered another explanation for what they did: *They gave many such orders to many people, in order to implicate as many as possible in their guilt.*[69] This has a ring of political truth to it, though Socrates may have been reluctant to draw attention to the role that his past association with some of the leaders might have played. Whatever the motives of the Thirty, they were wrong in thinking Socrates would obey: *That government, powerful as it was, did not frighten me into any wrongdoing. When we left the Hall, the other four went to Salamis and brought in Leon, but I went home.* Socrates took a risk in refusing to go along with the arrest – *I might have been put to death for this, had not the government fallen shortly afterwards* – and he emphasises the incontrovertible nature of his resistance: *There are many who will witness to these events.*[70]

Socrates was saved from the consequences of his disobedience because the Thirty Tyrants found themselves so unpopular that Sparta withdrew its military support rather than face a violent showdown. Anytus and others returned from exile to confront the Thirty outside Athens. In the fight that followed, Critias, Charmides and a number of their supporters were killed and only then did the King of Sparta step in to restore some stability. The outcome was that Sparta allowed the restoration of a democracy in 403, the outlawing of the leaders of the oligarchs who were still in Athens and, in a spirit of reconciliation designed to heal the political wounds, a general amnesty for those who supported the rule of the Thirty. The amnesty meant that no one could be made to answer charges relating to the political strife before 403 and people like Anytus, who had had property confiscated and sold when he fled from the Thirty Tyrants, did not attempt to recover it when he was back in Athens.

An amnesty, however, is not the same as amnesia, and Socrates' past association with people like Critias, Charmides and Alcibiades was not going to win him any friends in the restored democracy.

'Gentlemen of Athens, you executed Socrates the sophist, because he was clearly responsible for the education of Critias, one of the Thirty anti-democratic leaders.'

Aeschines, a leading Athenian orator of the mid-4th century.[71]

What kind of disgraceful theorising was this intellectual up to, people reasoned, when one of those he mixed with, and could well have influenced, turned into a corrupt dictator? Xenophon, seeking to exonerate Socrates, acknowledged the ill will to which Critias and Alcibiades exposed his friend, but downplayed Socrates' responsibility by saying that they used Socrates cynically and ignored the good he taught them. This seems like pleading in the face of the tacitly acknowledged fact that Socrates had suffered irreparable damage to his reputation, and to his chances of a fair trial, because of his political connections.

Knowing Critias and Alcibiades was certainly not to Socrates' advantage, but it is another step altogether to argue, as Aeschines did in the 4th century and others have done in recent times, that bringing Socrates to trial was first and foremost a politically motivated act. The argument runs as follows. Supporters of the restored democracy, regarding Socrates as a culpable, authoritarian ideologue, because of those with whom he has been on good terms in the past and because he did not flee Athens when the city was under the rule of the Thirty Tyrants, decide to punish him and at the same time send out a clear warning to other reactionaries. Accusing him directly of bearing some responsibility for the political crimes of the oligarchs is not possible because of the amnesty law. Instead,

Socrates dressed in an Athenian toga

they concoct vague accusations of religious unorthodoxy and corruption of the young as a cover for what all those involved know to be the real nature of the trial.[72] The charges against Socrates are kept general, with no specific acts of impiety mentioned or the names of individuals allegedly corrupted, because such charges are not the real motives of his prosecutors. There is circumstantial evidence for such a plot. It is perhaps suggestive that the charge of impiety echoed that against Alcibiades after the mutilation of the herms. Moreover, in Plato's *Apology*, although someone called Meletus is the official prosecutor, it is clear that Socrates identifies the man behind the charges as Anytus, none other than the democrat who helped depose Critias and who had lost property because of his democratic credentials. According to Xenophon, Anytus also had a personal grudge against Socrates because his son had been advised by the philosopher not to follow the occupation of his father – Anytus was a tanner by trade – and to take more care to avoid adopting a disreputable lifestyle.[73]

'Critias and Alcibiades were two of his intimate friends; and these were not only the most proliferate of mankind, but involved their country in the greatest misfortunes; for, as among the Thirty none was ever so cruel and rapacious as Critias; so, during the democracy, none was so audacious, so dissolute, or so insolent, as Alcibiades.'

Xenophon quoting criticism made against Socrates.[74]

The conspiracy theory is ultimately unsatisfactory. There was undoubtedly a political dimension to the trial, and the particular animosity of Anytus was probably a factor, but politics in this narrow sense cannot be the major explanation for what took place. Although the amnesty law forbade Socrates being prosecuted for political offences allegedly committed before 403, it would not have prevented the prosecution bringing up his political associations to blacken his character. Yet there is little evidence that this was done. There was also nothing preventing Socrates bringing up these past political associations if he thought they needed addressing directly. In his trial Socrates does claim that the actual charges against him are not the underlying reason for his indictment. He ridicules the charges of impiety and corruption and exposes them as poor excuses for prosecuting him – *I do not think, men of Athens, that it requires a prolonged defence to prove that I am not guilty of the charges in Meletus' deposition* – and acknowledges that this is not really what his trial is about – *On the other hand, you know that what I said earlier is true, that I am very unpopular with many people. This will be my undoing, if I am undone, not Meletus or Anytus but the slanders and envy of many people.*[75] However, in identifying his unpopularity in Athens as the root cause of his predicament, Socrates is not referring to deliberate political persecution. Political wrangling and intrigues took place after 403, but there were no purges. Socrates acknowledges that he is on trial because of who he is and the reputation he has acquired, yet it becomes clear that he is referring not to his political sympathies but to his reputation and activity as a philosopher. He goes on immediately to state that he does not regard his predicament as unique. Another philosopher, Plato, who was present at the trial of Socrates, seems to have left Athens before the execution and stayed away for 12 years. He may have taken to heart what Socrates was warning about, a narrowing of the intellectual horizon and the persecution of thinkers like himself, and decided that it was not wise to remain in the city.

It is a commonly accepted view that Socrates was a political reactionary, that his ideal state would have been an oligarchy or a benevolent despotism, and an extreme version of the conspiracy theory about his trial more or less takes this as a premise. Yet there is no firm evidence that Socrates was against democracy and quite a lot to affirm the opposite. He resisted the demand of the Thirty Tyrants to participate in the arrest of a democrat even though he was putting his own life at risk. During his trial Socrates refers to a life-long friend of his, Chaerephon, who was a well-known democrat and who went into exile because of the Thirty Tyrants and returned to fight in the civil war. Socrates' whole life was spent in democratic Athens, he served his city honourably and with distinction as a hoplite and, as mentioned earlier, when explaining why he will not escape from Athens to avoid execution, he speaks of a moral contract binding him to accept the laws of a city he respects. When Socrates imagines himself addressing a fellow citizen his finds himself saying *Good Sir, you are an Athenian, a citizen of the greatest city with the greatest reputation for both wisdom and power*,[76] which hardly seems indicative of someone opposed to the democracy of Athens. What distinguished Athens from other cities was its democratic constitution, rule of law and freedom of speech, and even though Socrates could admire Sparta and other non-democratic cities as well-governed, he chose to spend his life in Athens, a city whose democratic laws he respected to the point where he would accept the legitimacy of a death penalty imposed on him, enacted as it was in accordance with those laws.[77]

The idea that Socrates was against democracy comes partly from his philosophical discussions, where he draws attention more than once to the point that if someone possesses expert knowledge of a trade or a craft then one is inclined to listen to what they have to say, rather than follow the advice of someone with no professional knowledge. This point could be used as an argument by analogy for the idea that if someone possessed knowledge relating to ethics or politics, then they too ought to be obeyed. Put simply like this, it could be the basis of an argument against democracy and for the value of being governed by those who know what is best: *And certainly with actions just and unjust, shameful and beautiful, good and bad, about which we are now deliberating, should we follow the opinion of the many and fear it, or that of the one, if there is one who has knowledge of these things?*[78] This could be a theoretical justification for oligarchy but, as the final qualification makes clear, such an argument only holds if there is someone with this kind of knowledge. As will be seen, the whole thrust of Socrates' arguments is towards the realisation that no one actually possesses this kind of knowledge.

Socrates' enemy was not so much an individual like Anytus, or a group of democrats intent on revenge, as the anxious and fractured society he found himself in after the ordeal of the Peloponnesian War. In terms of the 5th-century Greek consciousness, the conflict had turned into a world war, one that went on gruellingly for nearly three decades, and at the end of it all Athens was on the losing side, beaten and humiliated. There had been a tremendous loss of life and material well-being, and the confidence and pride of the past had slowly burnt out in the fires of a 27-year-long conflict. In the original sense of the Greek word, it had been a holocaust, a burnt offering, and the self-belief of Athenians was reduced to embers. The Homeric ideals of warfare, if they ever existed outside of the epic imagination, became incongruous and irrelevant. War crimes and atrocities were committed on all sides: the slaughter on Melos by the Athenians and the mass killing of prisoners by Sparta after Aegospotami were not isolated events. Towards the end of the war Athens, frustrated by absconders from the fleet, voted to amputate the right hand of everyone caught attempting to desert. The war intensified emotions and prejudices, turning Socrates the eccentric intellectual into Socrates the irresponsible freethinker and atheist. In periods of stress and difficulty, anxieties can be relieved by pointing a finger at someone who is different.

On trial, at the beginning of his defence, Socrates is aware that his reputation is the source of his problems. *There have been many who have accused me to you for many years now, and none of their accusations are true. These I fear much more than I fear Anytus and his friends.*[79] He goes on to spell out exactly the kind of accusations he has faced over the years, allegations that have now hardened into serious legal charges: *It goes something like this: Socrates is guilty of wrongdoing in that he busies himself studying things in the sky and below the earth; he makes the worse into stronger argument, and he teaches these same things to others.*[80] The kind of person being described here would have been recognised by the jury as a Sophist, from the Greek word *sophia*, which was used to denote expertise in particular fields of knowledge as well as a more general sense of wisdom. It is in the sense of cleverness rather than wisdom that it became the term for peripatetic teachers who came to Athens in the second half of the 5th century. The origins of the Sophists lay with the 6th-century philosophers from Ionia who first began to speculate about the nature of the physical world. When Athens became the cultural and intellectual centre of the Greek world after the defeat of the Persians, the emphasis of thinkers who came to the city shifted to key questions about the relative merits of custom and convention, as opposed to nature, as a way of understanding the ethnological differences between the Greek and non-Greek worlds. A related aspect of this kind of debate was the question of what constituted excellence (*aretē*) in a particular field, and whether it was something innate or a quality that could be taught. It served the interests of aristocrats, of course, to believe that excellence was innate and hereditary, but in democratic Athens there was a market for those who could claim otherwise.

Emerging from this theoretical debate, some thinkers claimed to possess *sophia* and to be able to teach excellence to others. In Athens, where the spoken word and the ability to frame an argument was at the heart of Assembly debates, skills of rhetoric were highly prized because of their practical value. In the law courts, too, litigants and prosecutors had to plead their own cases – there were no lawyers just as there were no professional politicians – and clever arguments could win a law case just as they could advance a political career. There arose a class of teachers, the Sophists, who earned their living by charging for lessons in debating skills and the art of framing persuasive arguments. The power politics of Athens' participatory democracy made the skills and techniques they offered a valuable commodity and, like management gurus of today, they held out the promise of public success.

By the end of the 5th century, by which time most Sophists were dead, their reputation had been damaged. In the minds of traditionalists, they were responsible for having undermined sound moral values by using clever arguments that disregarded the truth and encouraging an ethical relativism that led to atheism. The rhetorical skills taught by Sophists enabled a persuasive speaker to convince a majority to follow a course of action that served their selfish interests but not necessarily those of the *polis*. This was one way of explaining the disastrous course of the war with Sparta. People like Alcibiades could be seen to have led people astray with their smart speeches and polished oratory. Athenian society, reeling from the tumultuous consequences of a disastrous war and seeking someone to blame for its wounds, made Socrates its scapegoat. To conservatives, he was a Sophist and

And watch, or the sophist might deceive us in advertising what he sells, the way merchants who market food for the body do. In general, those who market provisions don't know what is good or bad for the body – they just recommend everything they sell – nor do those who buy.

Socrates speaking in Plato, *Protagoras.*[81]

it was in this context that he was damaged by his past association with Alcibiades and Critias, because people thought it was from Socrates that they had learnt how to question and subvert traditional values that could have saved Athens.

Alcibiades had used an argument typical of the Sophists when supporting the case for an expedition to Sicily. Athens, he argued, had to take the war to Sicily: 'a city which is active by nature will soon ruin itself if it changes its nature and becomes idle' and Athenians would find happiness by 'accepting the character' they had.[82] Then, when Alcibiades turned himself over to the Spartans, he justified his act of betrayal with more sophistry – 'And the worst enemies of Athens are not those who, like you, have only harmed her in war, but those who have forced her friends to turn against her ... I am trying to recover a country that has ceased to be mine'[83] – claiming that he was the true patriot because he was prepared to aid Sparta in order to be able to return to Athens.

If the city was going to rebuild its identity and self-esteem, there was no place, social conservatives might have felt, for the likes of Socrates. The philosopher's enemies were those who labelled him a Sophist, an intellectual mercenary whose ethical relativism had helped undermine Athens. Knowing this to be the root cause of the prejudice against him, Socrates insists that he is not and never was a Sophist and that he has never been involved unjustly with *any one of those who they slanderously say are my pupils* – almost certainly a reference to Alcibiades and Critias – and that *If anyone, young or old, desires to listen to me when I am talking and dealing with my own concerns, I have never begrudged this to anyone, but I do not converse when I receive a fee and not when I do not.*[84] The phrasing of the last disclaimer may sound clumsy, but the translation is literal and it expresses the stark emphasis that Socrates is intent on making. He is not a Sophist and, for the second time in his defence speech – having earlier said that *if you have heard from anyone that I undertake to teach people and charge a fee for it, that is not true either*[85] – he denies ever having accepted payment for teaching. He is also adamant in disclaiming any suspicion that he nurtured anti-democrats like Alcibiades and Critias, emphasising that he freely engages with rich and poor alike and that *I cannot be held responsible for the good or bad conduct of these people, as I never promised to them anything and have not done so.*[86] Socrates knows that the jury he is addressing is predisposed to regard him as a Sophist and that it is difficult to identify a social prejudice with any one individual: *What is most absurd in all this is that one cannot even know or mention their names unless one of them is a writer of comedies.*[87] The writer of comedies is Aristophanes, the playwright who portrayed Socrates in his *Clouds*, perhaps affectionately, as a potty scientist with crack-brained ideas and as a morally subversive Sophist.

The plot of *Clouds* centres around the plight of an uneducated farmer, Strepsiades, who is suffering financially because of his son's expensive interest in horses. Unable to sleep with worry, he hopes that by paying for his son's attendance at a 'thinking school' or a 'logic factory' he will learn the kind of verbal tricks that will allow him to outwit his creditors. Socrates runs the school and when Strepsiades first encounters him he is ridiculously suspended above the ground in a basket, contemplating the heavens. Socrates is parodied as an unworldly buffoon who busies himself with such vital questions as from which end of its body a mosquito breaks wind. His gods are not the traditional deities but the Clouds, who appear as goddesses and who, as Socrates expounds, are the true controllers of the weather, not Zeus. Strepsiades comes to regret his plan when his son learns at the school how to produce an argument that justifies beating up one's parents, not the kind of sophistry he wanted to pay for. The play ends with the father setting fire to the school and the god Hermes appearing and justifying the righteous act of arson to Socrates because of 'all your blasphemies'.[88]

'A Logic factory
For the extra-clever. There are men there
Who can convince you heaven's a sort
Of fire-extinguisher all around us
And we're like cinders – yes, and they teach you
(If you pay enough) to win your arguments,
Whether you're right or wrong.'
Strepsiades to his son in Aristophanes' *Clouds*.[89]

What might have been enjoyed as a hilarious parody in 432 was also the beginning of a misleading image of Socrates as a Sophist, leading a 19th-century poet, Alphonse Lamartine, to accuse Aristophanes of being 'the first murderer of Socrates'.[90] In his defence speech, the philosopher himself is not so theatrical. While Socrates refers to Aristophanes as a source for the misleading impression that he is a Sophist, he also admits that his own style of philosophising is part of the problem he faces. Philosophy is the love of his life, he cannot abandon it at any price, but it has made him enemies and because of it he has acquired *much unpopularity, of a kind that is hard to deal with and is a heavy burden.*[91]

Part of the problem is that young men – *who follow me around of their own free will, those who have most leisure, the sons of the very rich* – have imitated his style of questioning and caused offence to others: *I think they find an abundance of men who believe they have some knowledge but know little or nothing. The result is that those whom they question are angry, not with themselves but with me.*[92] Philosophy – from *philos*, a friend, and *sophos*, wisdom – was Socrates' best friend, but the style in which he pursued it made him enemies of a fatal kind.

The Style of Socrates

Socrates insists that he has never received payment in return for his philosophy and, just as important in differentiating himself from the Sophists, he draws the jury's attention to the fact that he has never claimed to have any special knowledge that could be taught. In this sense he was not a teacher at all – *I have never been anyone's teacher*[93] – because the kind of moral excellence, virtue, that he was concerned with was not capable of being taught: *If only wisdom were like water, which always flows from a full cup into an empty one.*[94] For Socrates, virtue came from self-examination and from how one chose to conduct one's life and it was the oracle at Delphi that helped him appreciate the limited kind of wisdom he did possess – a wisdom so peculiar that it could never be packaged and sold as a product.

The oracle at Delphi, by delivering an answer to a question, allowed the ancient Greeks to engage in a form of dialogue with the god Apollo. It is thought that major consultations at Delphi took place nine times a year and they involved a question being put to a divinely-inspired woman, the *pythia*. Sitting in a sacred space at Delphi, the *pythia* entered a trance in which she was visited by Apollo and provided with an answer to the question. Sometime generally agreed to be around 430, a close friend of Socrates named Chaerephon journeyed to Delphi on the southern slopes of Mount Parnassus with a question about his philosopher friend. The oracle at Delphi could give famously ambiguous answers, but when

A dramatic depiction of the Oracle at Delphi

asked by Chaerephon if there was anyone wiser than Socrates the reply was a straightforward negative.[95] Both Plato and Xenophon report this story and, given that Plato has Socrates say that he can call upon the brother of the deceased Chaerephon as a witness, it seems unlikely to be fictional. If it took place around 430, Socrates would have been in his thirties, with another 25 or more years to go before his trial, and Aristophanes' *Clouds* yet to be produced on the stage.

Socrates did not take Apollo's laconic reply at face value: *I asked myself: 'Whatever does the god mean? What is his riddle?'*[96] In one sense there was no riddle because the god meant just what he said: there was no one wiser than Socrates. In another sense, the oracle was unusually cryptic because only by subjecting it to a test would its truth be revealed. Socrates, thinking he could hardly be the wisest of all, set out to find someone wiser than himself and thereby refute the oracle; but after questioning a public figure with a reputation for wisdom – *I thought that he appeared wise to many people and especially to himself, but he was not*[97] – he found he had to keep searching. He adopted a more systematic approach by examining representative members of groups usually thought wise but in the process found himself getting unpopular and, at the same time, surprised by what unfolded: *I found that those who had the highest reputation were nearly the most deficient, while those who were thought to be inferior were more knowledgeable.*[98] In the end, Socrates comes to see that what Apollo meant was not that he was really wiser than everyone else but that some people, like himself, can lay claim to a limited of degree of wisdom only because they do not delude themselves about their knowledge. His only claim to a kind of wisdom rested with his epistemological modesty.

What Socrates says about Apollo's response at Delphi is that: *His oracular response meant that human wisdom is worth little or nothing, and that when he says this man, Socrates, he is using my name as an example, as if he said, 'This man among you, mortals, is wisest who, like Socrates, understands that his wisdom is worthless.'*

By the time of Lucian, writing over 200 years later, the import of the oracle's reply has been reduced to something less nuanced and more dogmatic: 'Socrates ... used to proclaim to all and sundry that so far from knowing absolutely everything he knew absolutely nothing – or nothing except the fact that he knew nothing.'[99]

By requiring Socrates to question the nature of the god's reply in order for its truth to be constituted, the oracle at Delphi remained idiosyncratically true to its reputation for riddles. The early philosopher from Ionia, Heraclitus, had said, 'The lord whose oracle is in Delphi neither speaks out nor conceals but gives a sign',[100] and this is how Socrates responded to his pronouncement. He took Apollo's oracle as a sign to engage in conversation with those who think they are wise: *Then if I do not think he is, I come to the assistance of the god and show him that he is not wise.*[101]

Socrates' style, therefore, is not to write books of philosophy or deliver speeches on philosophical themes, but to talk and listen to people. He seeks, negatively, to deconstruct the reasoning people use to justify their lives and, positively, to explore through conversation the principles by which one could live a happy and fulfilling life – and he goes out into the ordinary world of 5th-century Athens in order to do this, engaging in pavement interviews, but with no leaflets to dispense, no membership to take up and seeking to collect no money. He becomes a familiar figure on the streets of Athens, in the marketplace, shops, gymnasia and the workshops of craftsmen, conversing with young and old, rich and not-so-rich and unsettling the suburbs of their minds by summoning them to examine their existence and the consistency of their beliefs.

We will never know exactly what these conversations were like, but what seems certain is that they made a deep impression on at least some of those who experienced them. The Socratic dialogues of Plato and the *Memoirs* and other writings of Xenophon are the texts that have survived out of a far larger genre of writing inspired by the conversations of Socrates and even these two are far from presenting us with the same impression of the philosopher's style. The manner of the incisive and ironic intellectual portrayed in Plato's texts may belong no more to the 'real' Socrates than does the homely and conventional portrait of Xenophon's Socrates.

Nietzsche saw no difficulty in accepting a Socrates whose mode of living could encompass both these very different portraits and today, when Xenophon's accounts of Socrates are rated as less reliable or revealing than Plato's, it is worth considering Nietzsche's contention that 'If all goes well, the time will come when one will take up [Xenophon's] *Memorabilia* [*Memoirs*] of Socrates rather than the Bible as a guide to morals and reason.'[102]

Socrates distinguishes between the kind of knowledge he seeks but fails to find, that relating to moral excellence and the good life, and the kind of knowledge possessed by craftsmen. He does not deny that they possess knowledge of their craft – *they knew things I did not know, and to that extent they were wiser than I* – but, ironically, because of their particular mastery in a certain craft they made the mistake of thinking they are equally knowledgeable in other areas of life *and this error of theirs overshadowed the wisdom they had, so that I asked myself, on behalf of the oracle, whether I should prefer to be as I am, with neither their wisdom nor their ignorance, or to have both. The answer I gave myself and the oracle was that it was to my advantage to be as I am.*[104] What Socrates is seeking is a kind of skill in ethical areas of life comparable to the kind of skill possessed by craftsmen in their individual crafts, skill that would guarantee a virtuous life. What he comes to appreciate is

'Socrates was almost continually in men's sight. The first hours of the morning were usually spent in the places set apart for walking, or the public exercises; and from thence he went to the forum, at the time when the people were accustomed to assemble ... As for himself, man, and what related to man, were the only subjects on which he chose to employ himself. To this purpose, all his enquiries and conversation turned upon what was pious, what impious; what honourable, what base; what just, what unjust; what wisdom, what folly; what courage, what cowardice; what a state or political community ... '

Xenophon, *Memoirs*.[103]

the elusiveness of such knowledge, although he does not cease from seeking it, and he has no time for those Sophists who brazenly assert they possess and can therefore teach and transmit knowledge of the good life.

In showing a person's lack of wisdom, Socrates is not being patronising or didactic because the lack of wisdom is mutual, and when he inquires into the nature of something, asking what is 'courage' or 'friendship' or 'piety', the question is a genuine one. The Socrates problem is a factor here because in the later works of Plato, such as the *Republic*, the character of Socrates is used to advance an argument and lead the discussion towards a conclusive and positive moment of clarity. In the early works, the Socratic Dialogues, such states of clarity have only a negative quality, the conversation reaching a point where the basis for what seemed to be a claim for knowledge is removed. Aristotle was aware of this – 'This was why Socrates posed questions without answering them; he admitted his lack of knowledge'[105] – and the characteristic cross-examination that is recognisable as the Socratic method in both Plato and Xenophon, the 'elenchus' as it is known, works to expose the true ignorance that lies behind claims to certain knowledge.

The elenchus is seen clearly at work in Plato's *Euthyphro*, set in the agora outside the magistrate's office where Socrates has been called to answer the charges of impiety that will result in his trial and execution. There he meets Euthyphro, who has laid a charge of murder against his own father for the death of a servant. A charge against one's own father was an extraordinary and outrageous act that could itself be viewed as impious. The circumstances of the servant's death are such that Euthyphro's father may, at worst, be responsible for manslaughter, but the righteous son, whose name means 'straight thinker', is determined to pursue a charge of murder. The stage is set for Socrates to ask Euthyphro to define the nature of piety, the 'What is x?' question that forms the opening move in the elenchus, though the conversation is initiated by

Euthyphro and not Socrates. At first Euthyphro thinks that merely by pointing to his behaviour in charging his father – acting to prosecute wrongdoers regardless of their relationship to you – he can demonstrate the nature of piety. He then enlists the myth of Zeus imprisoning his own father Cronus in his support, because, he argues, people think Zeus is just and in principle his legal action is of the same order. Socrates gets Euthyphro to admit that the prosecution of his father is not the only example of piety and that therefore a more general definition is required. Euthyphro then comes up with what he thinks is a better definition, that 'what is dear to the gods is pious, what is not is impious.'[106]

The next typical stage in the Socratic method is to point out inconsistencies in the proposed definition and so Socrates reminds Euthyphro that, as shown by the myth he himself cited, the gods do not always agree amongst themselves. Zeus, who imprisoned Cronus, might see the justice of Euthyphro's prosecution of his father, but Cronus, who is also a god, would not be willing to approve of such a principle. Given the likelihood of disagreement between the gods, the definition cannot hold. Euthyphro then accepts what seems a tighter definition, offered this time by Socrates, that whatever all the gods hate is impiety and whatever all the gods love is piety. To bring the argument up to date in a monotheistic world, we might think of different religions instead of different gods. Then Socrates asks an artfully simple question: *Is the pious being loved by the gods because it is pious, or is it pious because it is being loved by the gods?*[107]

'Euthyphro: I would certainly say that the pious is what all the gods love, and the opposite, what all the gods hate, is the impious.

Socrates: *Then let us again examine whether this is a sound statement, or do we let it pass, and if one of us, or someone else, merely says that something is so, do we accept that it is so? Or should we examine what the speaker means?*

Euthyphro: We must examine it, but I certainly think that this is now a fine statement.

Socrates: *We shall soon know better whether it is. Consider this: Is the pious being loved by the gods because it is pious, or is it pious because it is being loved by the gods?*[108]

To say something is pious because it is loved by the gods does not help in understanding the nature of piousness: it only invites us to ask why the gods love this something rather than something else. To say instead, as Euthyphro does in reply to Socrates' question, that piety is loved by the gods because it is pious is true merely by definition and so adds nothing of substance to our understanding of piety. So Euthyphro's attempt to explain the nature of what he feels so sure about understanding has failed again. Socrates' argument is just as valid in a monotheistic world because he has shown that any attempt to understand the nature of what is morally good in terms of what God desires or commands is not going to take us very far. God's approval does not make a thing good: we think God approves it *because* it is good. The question of what goodness is, *why* we think a thing good, cannot be answered, therefore, merely by pointing to God's approval of it. Socrates, whose philosophic mission originates in Apollo, does not look to religion in the task of seeking to care for his soul.

Euthyphro, so blithely sure of why he was prosecuting his father, is bewildered as a result of having to explain and justify his beliefs and this is when Socrates humourously compares himself to his ancestor Daedalus. The skill of Daedalus in inventing mechanical devices was regarded as a superhuman ability to make statues move; and some of his statues, it was said, needed tying down to prevent them walking away.[109] Socrates says that if he was the one putting forward arguments of the kind advanced by the self-assured Euthyphro then *you would perhaps be making fun of me and say that because of my kinship with him my conclusions in discussion run away and will not stay where one puts them.*[110] In this sense,

Socrates admits, he is indeed like Daedalus, for just as the famed inventor brought movement to his mechanical devices and statues, he, Socrates, introduces flux into Euthyphro's seemingly firm arguments. The irony is that Socrates is looking for solid foundations, seeking to find a secure basis for claims about morality: *I would rather have your statements to me remain unmoved than possess the wealth of Tantalus as well as the cleverness of Daedalus.*[111] As much as he might like the security of a prescriptive definition, and as much as the attempt to pin down an unassailable definition is typical of Socrates' style, it is just as characteristic that he never actually achieves this. Socrates is not practising sophistry in exposing the confusion and ignorance at the heart of Euthyphro's claims, he is merely bringing to light what has not been clearly seen. Yet it is easy to imagine that those whose claims to knowledge were exposed in this way might have repaired their damaged egos by dismissing the philosopher as a devious Sophist.

Plato presents Euthyphro with heavy-handed irony as exceptionally vain and shallow. Although discombobulated by his conversation with Socrates, he is protected by a lack of self-knowledge that prevents him from learning or changing as a result of the experience. He does not reconsider the moral propriety of prosecuting his father in the way that he does. Blinded by his arrogance, he makes an excuse when Socrates seeks to pursue further their inquiry into the nature of piety: *Some other time, Socrates, for I am in a hurry now, and it is time for me to go.*[112] Like a character in a Jane Austen story, his conceit and self-delusion is a suit of armour that cannot be pierced by rationality or reflection and, as with an Austen novel, space is created for readers to ask themselves if they too have ways of shielding themselves from the ethical implications of the characters' conversations.

Euthyphro is not the only character who engages in conversation with Socrates but who emerges unchanged by the experience. In *Charmides*, Critias and Charmides assume that they have an understanding of the nature of the moral virtue of temperance; but as with the other Socratic dialogues, the conversation in the text only serves to reveal their confusion. Although *Charmides* has a positive conclusion, with Charmides willingly accepting his guardian Critias' instruction to continue investigating the nature of temperance with Socrates, such good intentions are later negated by the very intemperate actions of Charmides and Critias as leaders of the Thirty Tyrants following the defeat of Athens in the Peloponnesian War.

It is because Socrates is not a teacher, because he does not know for himself the nature of moral excellence, that he cannot take the praise or the blame for what happens to those who join him in philosophical conversations. Socrates' style is that of a facilitator: he hopes to enable learning and self-discovery to take place, but the outcome depends on the contribution of his interlocutor: *If anyone says that he has learned anything from me, or that he heard anything privately that the others did not hear, be assured that he is not telling the truth.*[113] It is a radically new kind of learning, one that changes the manner in which your life is conducted, because so much of what passes for knowledge is shown to be superficial, mere opinion, and what is left is the learner's decision whether to act or not on the basis of this new awareness. Xenophon has a character, Hippias, criticise Socrates for not being willing to answer a simple question about the nature of justice. The reply to Hippias is: *If I don't reveal my views on justice in words, I do so by my conduct.*[114] In the end it does not come down to what is said about beliefs and values; what matters is how one lives: *I care nothing for what most people care about: money-making, administration of property, generalships, success in public debates … I did not choose that path, but rather the one by which I could do the greatest good to each of you in particular: by trying to persuade each of you to concern himself less about what he has than about what he* is, *so that he may make himself as good and as reasonable as possible.*[115]

This shifting of existential responsibility onto the individual is revolutionary, and it could discomfort 5th-century citizens just as it could 21st-century ones. One of Xenophon's anecdotes ends with Socrates' interlocutor, Euthedemus, reduced to silence after a conversation on ethical issues which leaves him confused and uncertain about what to think. *But it was not Euthedemus alone to whom Socrates gave that sort of uneasiness: many who were once his followers, had forsaken him on that account.*[116] Socrates calls upon those he converses with to take ethical care of themselves: not just to talk the talk about moral excellence,

'You don't appear to me to know that whoever comes into close contact with Socrates and associates with him in conversation must necessarily, even if he began by conversing about something quite different in the first place, keep on being led about by the man's arguments until he submits to answering questions about himself concerning both his present manner of life and the life he has lived hitherto.'

Plato, *Laches*.[119]

but to conduct their lives in such a way as to render their talk meaningful. In the last analysis, *aretē* (virtue) cannot satisfactorily be defined or taught because it must be lived by the individual. Socrates knows that he can cause anxiety in those he questions: *They do say that I am a very odd sort of person, always causing people to get into difficulties. You must have heard that, surely?*[117] The difficulty that Socrates creates arises from the originality of his philosophical style and it is this originality, seemingly inseparable from his unique character and personality, that Plato has Alcibiades praise in the *Symposium*. Socrates, explains Alcibiades, is special because there is no obvious way of comparing his character and style with someone else's. We can form an idea of what Achilles was like, he says, by looking at the achievements of other great warriors or the renowned Spartan general Brasidas. There is a parallel for most people but not for Socrates: *But this man here is so bizarre, his ways and his ideas are so unusual, that, search as you might, you'll never find anyone else, alive or dead, who's even remotely like him.*[118]

A portrait of Artemis by Louis Prion from the Salon of 1911

We learn that Socrates' mother was a midwife in the course of his own attempt to explain his philosophical style. He says how his dialectical method, the elenchus, is similar to that of his mother's skill in midwifery, only that he attends the birth of a new consciousness, not that of a baby, hoping to be of some practical help. The analogy, he explains, is a useful one in other respects because, just as a virgin was the goddess of midwives, he himself is barren of wisdom: *I cannot claim as the child of my own soul any discovery worth the name of wisdom.*[120] What he can do is to assist others to reach a point where they can see the inadequacy of their presumed claims to understanding and hope that from that point on they will set about creating for themselves a new kind of understanding. This *maieutic* method proceeds along the lines shown in the *Euthyphro*, starting with an attempt at definition,

Artemis, the twin sister of Apollo, was a virgin goddess who roamed the open countryside hunting wild animals but also, paradoxically, overseeing their safety. Equally puzzling is the fact that she was childless but associated with birth and reproduction, and one of her titles was 'nurse of youths'. A divine midwife, she watched over women in labour, who called to her in their birth-pangs.

often after the interlocutor has begun by merely listing examples of the concept under discussion, and then advancing to a subsequent definition which is shown to be as inadequate as the first one. Sometimes three or even four definitions are offered before the dialogue breaks down because no apparent progress has been made. *Socrates, before I even met you I used to hear that you are always in a state of perplexity and that you bring others to the same state.*[121]

Socrates is sincere in saying that when it comes to moral excellence he does not have the certain, technical kind of knowledge that craftsmen possess, nor does he have the demonstrable kind of knowledge that can be deduced from self-evident principles, of the kind that mathematics can reveal. What he does have is a set of ethical convictions which he is prepared to defend in verbal arguments and in the way he conducts his life and deals with other people. What matters to Socrates is the care of the *psuchē*, a word that is translated as soul (in Latin, *psychē*) but in a way that can be very misleading owing to the modern, theological connotations of the term. Plato confuses matters by using the character of Socrates in his non-Socratic dialogues to argue for the immortality of the soul, something about which the historical Socrates was most likely agnostic. In ancient Greek thought, *psuchē* does not have a single meaning, but it signifies a set of non-bodily qualities which overlap with terms of ours like will, desire, consciousness, intellect, and the spirit of a person, even including their personality and how they live. It is what distinguishes an animate being from inanimate matter and, metaphorically, *psuchē* can stand for those things we hold as dear as life and everything that makes someone more than just a physical organism. It is what Yeats called 'the deep heart's core' and what Nietzsche saw as 'the oldest and most venerable of hypotheses' once its theological accretions are removed.[122]

Socrates brings an ethical and existential dimension to the soul, realigning the Delphic precept 'know thyself', which traditionally referred to knowing one's limits as a mortal and avoiding hubris, to posit the importance of self-reflection and right conduct: *So the command that we should know ourselves means we should know our souls.*[123] For Socrates, taking care of your soul becomes the conduct of life, the art of existence, and involves looking into yourself, your own being, and accounting for who you are. The Sophists, who cannot know or teach what is best for someone else, only offer cosmetic qualities. In *Protagoras*, where Socrates compares Sophists to merchants who will always claim that what they have to sell is the best available product, he says that if you buy food from a greengrocer you can have it examined by an expert if you suspect it may be bad for your body, but the same cannot be done with what the Sophist peddles. *You put down your money and take the teaching away in your soul by having learned it, and off you go, either helped or injured.*[124] In the absence of an expert, you must look to yourself and give clear reasons for your conduct, examining the inferences and refining or rejecting possible definitions.

Socrates wants people to be self-sufficient and autonomous in matters of moral excellence and this is what he demonstrates in his own life. It does not mean being apolitical – quite the opposite: it carries a heavy responsibility and the risk of conflict with the State. Socrates learned this to his cost when his soul obliged him to oppose those who, illegally and unjustly, wanted to put on trial together the generals accused of failing to pick up survivors and the dead after the battle of Arginusae. In the same way, he had to oppose the Thirty Tyrants when they summoned him to assist in the arrest of a political opponent.

Taking care of your soul can be a risky business because it entails trusting yourself and doing what you think is right, whatever other people may think. He explains the risks to his jury: *Be sure, men of Athens, that if I had long ago attempted to take part in politics, I should have died long ago, and benefited neither you nor myself. Do not be angry with me for speaking the truth; no man will survive who genuinely opposes you or any other crowd and prevents the occurrence of many unjust and illegal happenings in the city.*[125] Socrates is not being anti-democratic or apolitical, but he is acknowledging the difficulty of reconciling his concern for moral excellence with the nature of the crowd. *A man who really fights for justice must lead a private, not a public, life if he is to survive for even a short time.*[126] He makes the same point in the *Gorgias*, explaining how he cannot philosophize with large groups of people.[127] So he wrote nothing himself: those who came after him and sought to preserve his memory chose to present his ideas in the form of dialogues.

The enduring interest of Socrates lies in his philosophy, but as with Wittgenstein, another strange and hugely original thinker, the philosophy and the man are inseparable. Neither individual saw his philosophy as something detached, or detachable, from the way he conducted his life, from momentous life-changing choices to day-to-day matters like how to dress. Both astonished their friends by the kind of decisions they made in important matters, and both were uncompromisingly philosophical in everything they did. There is another remarkable similarity between Socrates and Wittgenstein because in both cases their way of coming at a philosophical issue, their philosophical stance, *is*, in a very important sense, their philosophy. There are not *-isms* that neatly label their philosophies because what interests them is how to go about inquiring into a problem, not the nature of the outcome. Wittgenstein and Socrates both thought that why we do something is just as important, and sometimes more important, than what we do.

Wittgenstein comes at an issue by asking 'How is language being used here?' Socrates asks 'How well do we know ourselves here?' Socrates' fundamental assumption, then, is that the good life must be founded on self-knowledge, that it is only by examining ourselves that we can decide what is right. Given that Socrates is emphatic about the impossibility of certain knowledge in this sphere, how can he make such a big assumption? In the *Gorgias*, discussing an idea he derives from this founding principle, he says *I don't know how these things are, but no one I've ever met, as in this case, can say anything else without being ridiculous.*[128] That is, the principle remains provisional, like all of his knowledge: he presents it as a working assumption, valid until proven otherwise. It seems to be founded on his instincts about the way people are, but he does not want his assertions to be taken as a claim to wisdom.

His style can seem austerely intellectual, ignoring weakness of the will, passion, impetuosity and blind irrationality, so that while the insistence on self-examination and caring for one's soul may work for someone with Socrates' strength of character, it may seem a supremely weak foundation for a philosophy. This view of Socrates, however, is built on the assumption that reason and passion must conflict, an assumption that he rejects. He sees reason as something that is lived, something that is felt in the soul, and without passion and idealism it is pointlessly abstract; similarly, intellect cannot be kept separate from will. Irrational behaviour is not a mystery but rather something that arises because we do not know ourselves well enough. Knowledge, or the closest we can come to knowledge in the ethical sphere, has a necessary corollary in right conduct: it is impossible to know what is right and voluntarily, willfully do what is wrong. Aristotle says this is Socrates' position and Diogenes Laertius makes the same point: 'And it was a saying of his that there was one only good, namely knowledge; and one only evil, namely ignorance.'[129] Put simplistically like this, such a position seems easy to refute by pointing to cases of willed nastiness[130] – they are not hard to find. People behave in ways that are morally wrong and apparently they know that they are doing wrong. For Socrates, however, this is only because they have a mistaken idea of what is good for their soul. Socrates similarly argues that doing wrong back to someone who has unjustly hurt you is not in your soul's best interests because in doing wrong, however understandable it might seem, you damage your own soul. Out of self-interest, not altruism, acts of revenge, spitefulness or begrudgery are to be avoided.

What Socrates does acknowledge is the way group behaviour and the psychology of the crowd make it difficult to look into yourself and do what is right. Unfortunately, at the age of 70, Socrates was forced to deal with a crowd mentality when he found himself facing a jury of 500 men. It was in the spring of the year 399 and Athens was in a parlous state, recovering from a traumatic defeat in war and the throes of a violent tyranny that came in its wake. Could Socrates' unique style cope with the task of persuading a majority of 500 that he was not a irreligious freethinker, a possible threat to the future stability and well-being of the *polis* and someone who ought to be silenced?

Trial and Execution

The trial of Socrates lasted one day, as was common practice in 5th-century Athens for cases involving the death penalty, and the jury of male citizens over the age of thirty was chosen by lottery from a list of 6,000 jurors. The list was drawn up at the beginning of each year when volunteers were called to put themselves forward and earn a payment for each day they served. The rate of pay, three obols, was less than the average pay for a day's work and in *Wasps* Aristophanes mocks the fact that men too old for work make up a disproportionate element of a jury. Any citizen had recourse to Athenian law if they felt they had been personally wronged but it was also possible for citizens to bring a public action on behalf of the *polis*, risking the mandatory imposition of a financial penalty if they failed to obtain at least one-fifth of the jury's votes. A man named Meletus and his supporters were prepared to take this risk when they began legal proceedings against Socrates on behalf of the city.

Meletus would have gone to see the relevant magistrate, in this case the one responsible for charges relating to religion, presented to him a written indictment and sought his agreement that there was substance to the charge being made. The magistrate having accepted the grounds for a case, it was then Meletus' task to inform Socrates of the charge made against him and the need to appear before the magistrate at a specified date. On the set date, accuser and accused would see the magistrate and formal proceedings would be made public by the posting of the charge on a notice board in the agora. It was only at a subsequent hearing with the magistrate that Socrates would have entered his not-guilty plea and a date for trial established after the magistrate had heard statements from both parties. The size of the jury could vary but it was normally in the hundreds and in this case the number was set at 500.

'Meletus, the son of Meletus of Pittea, impeaches Socrates, the son of Sophroniscus, of Alopece: Socrates is guilty, inasmuch as he does not believe in the Gods whom the city worships, but introduces other strange deities; he is also guilty, inasmuch as he corrupts the young men, and the punishment he has incurred is death.'[131] Diogenes Laertius makes the astonishing statement that this indictment against Socrates was still on view in Athens in his own time, some 600 years after the trial.

The location of the building where Socrates stood trial is not known for certain but the educated guess is the southeastern corner of the agora, close to the bottom of the Acropolis. It had to be a large building to accommodate 500 jurors seated on wooden benches and a platform at the front where they were addressed by those involved in the case. There were no lawyers in Athenian law courts but accusers and defendants could pay a professional speech-writer and memorise the speech for delivery to the jury. Diogenes Laertius says the orator Lysias wrote a defence for Socrates but that he declined to use it; Plato has Socrates speak for himself: *spoken at random and expressed in the first words that come to mind, for I put my trust in the justice of what I say.*[132] Accusers and defendants could also call on witnesses as part of their presentation.

The trial was divided into three parts, beginning early in the morning with the prosecution presenting its case and with the afternoon devoted to the defence. Equal time was allotted to both parties and measured by a clay water clock. There were no standards of evidence or guidance given to the jury, no obligation for them to feel that the charges had been established beyond a reasonable doubt. There was no judge, only a court official in charge of the water clock and the voting procedure, and the public could gather freely around the contestants. Interjections from the public or even jury members were not uncommon, especially in a controversial case, and it is likely that the trial of Socrates was attended by an above-average crowd of spectators and interested individuals. There are no records of the prosecution case, made by Meletus and two others, Anytus and Lycon, but accounts of Socrates' defence by Plato and Xenophon have survived and of these two, Plato's is regarded as the most reliable, for he was present at the trial and Xenophon was not; and it is certainly the most arresting.

Socrates begins his defence by pointing to the long-standing prejudice that mistakenly identifies him as a philosopher who proposes naturalistic explanations for what happens in nature – *studying things in the sky and below the earth* – and who goes about making *the worse into the stronger argument*.[133] Socrates refers to the play by Aristophanes, performed over 20 years earlier, indicating that he is aware of having carried for a long time the reputation of being a freethinking atheist who questions traditional theology. Denying such accusations, Socrates challenges anyone in the jury to speak up if he has ever heard him talking in this way.

Socrates explains how such a misunderstanding has arisen by saying that he does possess a kind of wisdom but not the kind that the Sophists claim to be able to teach. In order to explain this to his jury, he announces dramatically: *I shall call upon the god at Delphi as witness to the existence and nature of the wisdom, if it be such.*[134] This leads him to recount the story of his friend's visit to the oracle at Delphi and Apollo's confirmation that there is no one wiser than Socrates. In the process of investigating the oracle's response, Socrates explains what he came to realise about his peculiar kind of wisdom. He tells the jury how he questioned politicians and realised they only *thought* they knew something, and how he questioned poets only to realise that while they possessed insights they could not explain or interpret wisely their knowledge. He then examined craftsmen, who obviously possessed knowledge of their craft, only to realise there was a downside to their knowledge that ultimately undermined the value of what they did know: *Each of them, because of his success at his craft, thought himself very wise in other most important pursuits, and this error of theirs overshadowed the wisdom they had.*[135] Socrates is different, he says, because he knows that he lacks wisdom of the *other most important pursuits* and it is only his awareness of his ignorance that gives him wisdom of a certain, limited kind.

Socrates explains all this because he wants to draw attention to the root causes of his unpopularity before cross-examining Meletus over his specific charges. He does not deny that his method of questioning can cause discomfort and he acknowledges that sons of the rich may follow him around and seek to imitate his style. In doing so, they irritate others and *the result is that those whom they question are angry, not with themselves but with me.*[136] This is the background that Socrates wants to draw to the jurors' attention before he deals with the actual charges brought against him.

There are three charges: (1) not believing in the gods of the polis, (2) believing in other kinds of spirit and (3) corrupting the city's youth. Charge (1) is a consequence of (2) – Socrates believes in other spirits instead of the city's gods – and together they lead to (3). All three charges are a subset of the unstated charge of atheism and Socrates brings this to the fore in his cross-examination of Meletus: *{Do} you mean that I teach the belief that there are some gods – and therefore I myself believe that there are gods and am not altogether an atheist … ? Or… that I do not believe in gods at all, and this is what I teach to others.*[137] Meletus, in confirming that he is accusing Socrates of outright atheism, is following the general defamation that has dogged the philosopher from his earliest days. Socrates began his defence by going back to the days of Aristophanes' play because the seeds of slander were sown over two decades earlier:

Those who spread that rumour, gentlemen, are my dangerous accusers, for their hearers believe that those who study these things do not even believe in the gods.[138]

The charge of atheism was a serious one and according to Plutarch, though writing 500 years after the trial, a decree had been passed at the beginning of the Peloponnesian War making atheism an indictable offence. It is not certain if anyone was prosecuted under this law but a number of such heresy trials may have taken place over the next 30 years against the leading intellectuals of Athens.[139] Whatever the extent of the anti-intellectualism, there was a reaction against the liberalism of pre-war Athens and Socrates feels his predicament to be the result of this. He thus proceeds to cross-examine Meletus with the intention of showing him to be acting irresponsibly by bringing such a charge against him.

Given that accusation (3) is built upon (1) and (2), Socrates asks Meletus who, then, is responsible for the proper, non-corrupting education of the city's youth. Meletus answers that the members of the jury, the trial audience, the citizen body as a whole, educates the youth – everyone fulfils their duty in this respect except Socrates. The absurdity of this claim seems clear and Socrates points to the silliness of thinking one person could corrupt the city's youth when everyone else is going about improving them. Socrates stays on the attack, exposing contradictions in Meletus' position by asking him whether he really believes that Socrates does not regard the sun and moon as gods. What was intended to be a rhetorical riposte is squarely batted back by Meletus, who claims Socrates says the sun is a stone and the moon only earth. How ridiculous, reasons the accused, for men to pay a Sophist – for Socrates is seen as a Sophist – for this kind of teaching when books by Anaxagoras espousing just such theories are readily and cheaply available.

Socrates continues his case against the credibility of Meletus' charge with a series of short analogies. Someone who believes in the activities of humans must believe in humans, and one who believes in horse activities or flute activities must accept the existence of horses or flutes. It follows that anyone who believes in *spiritual activities* must believe in spirits. As Meletus has charged him with (2) believing in other kinds of spirit, he concludes that *if I believe in spiritual things I must quite inevitably believe in spirits*.[140] Meletus reluctantly accepts that spirits are either gods themselves or the offspring of gods and, whatever is the case, it follows that Socrates cannot be an atheist.

Even though Socrates feels it is easy to expose the lack of logic and

The Greek philosopher Anaxagoras (500–428) came from Ionia but settled in Athens, where he became a friend of Pericles and remained for 30 years. He was charged with impiety, perhaps as a way of attacking Pericles, because of his theory that the sun is a red-hot stone. Such an explanation, denying the role of Helios the sun god, was enough to warrant prosecution. It seems that he fled Athens before the trial and settled in Asia Minor. The author of one book, now lost, what we know about Anaxagoras is based on references to him by later writers.

clear thinking in Meletus' case, he ends his cross-examination by returning to the remark he made at the very start of his defence. He does not feel that a formal rebuttal of the charges is sufficient to dislodge the prejudices that have built up against him. At first he qualifies his despair by focusing on the possibility of an acquittal – the prejudices against him *will be my undoing, if I am undone* – but he ends on a fatalistic note: *This has destroyed many other good men and will, I think, continue to do so. There is no danger that it will stop at me.*[141]

Despite, or because of, such misgivings, Socrates begins an uncompromising defence of the philosophical life. It is a mistake, he argues, to consider the risk of life or of death as more important than the issue of whether one is acting justly or unjustly – and he tells a story from the life of Achilles to support his point. The goddess Thetis, the mother of Achilles, told her son at Troy that if he returned to battle to avenge the slaying of his friend Patroclus then it would be his fate immediately to die. Socrates quotes his defiant response, *'Let me die at once,'* he said, *'when once I have given the wrongdoer his deserts, rather than remain here, a laughingstock by the curved ships, a burden upon the earth.' Do you think he gave thought to death and danger?*[142] Socrates, as committed to his life as a philosopher as Achilles was to his course of action, finds in the world of Troy a way of explaining what he is about. He makes the warrior hero of Homer a model for his own behaviour as a philosopher. It is difficult to know if the jury were enlightened by the analogy or shocked by the audacity of a comparison that reflects on the heroism of Achilles in this way.

The golden age of 5th-century Greece looked back to the age of Troy through the epic poems of Homer. There it found heroes like Achilles and Ajax, warriors who strove for individual honour in a culture where the good was understood not in our moral sense but in terms of martial prowess and personal courage. The cultivation of a reputation for these qualities defined success and virtue.

Socrates provides another analogy to explain his philosophic mission by reminding his jury that when a soldier is ordered to stay at his post then he does so without fear of the danger he faces. He recalls his own military service at Potidaea, Amphipolis and Delium in this respect and explains that, just as he was dutiful then, now he is carrying out the orders of the god Apollo who, through his oracle at Delphi, made it clear that Socrates should be a philosopher *to examine myself and others.*[143] He will not abandon this mission, whatever the cost or danger, even if he were to be released on the condition that he cease philosophising. He goes on to explain how the nature of his mission entails him asking fellow-citizens: *Are you not ashamed of your eagerness to possess as much wealth, reputation and honours as possible, while you do not care for nor give thought to wisdom or truth, or the best possible state of your soul?* He will pursue this question with anyone he meets and reproach those who attach *little importance to the most important things and greater importance to inferior things*.[144] The pursuit of money and fame as an end in itself, at the cost of caring for what is good, is foolish because it does not guarantee happiness. The moral excellence that brings happiness does not come from wealth and fame. It is the other way around: moral excellence brings a consciousness of what is really useful for one's happiness and this allows one to use money sensibly in the course of living well.

Socrates then addresses the jury, arguing that the city of Athens should be grateful for his service. In stirring people's complacency and shaming them into examining and improving their own lives, Socrates compares himself to a gadfly who stings a well-bred but sluggish horse into action. This is when he explains why he has not entered political life in a more public way, and how his divine sign (*daimonion*) warns him against taking part in public affairs. He goes on to mention his part in the trial of the ten generals after the battle of Arginusae and his defiance of the Thirty after the coup as examples of his commitment to doing what is right. He insists that he has never acted as a bad influence *with any one of those who they slanderously say are my pupils* and this remark, coming straight after his defiance of the Thirty, could be a response to the allegation that he was an associate of Critias and influenced his development.[145] Critias is not mentioned by name, nor is Alcibiades, but their association with Socrates could support the accusation that he has corrupted the city's youth. Perhaps this is what is in his mind when he invites anyone to come forward – or a relative of any such person – who could claim to have been corrupted by him. No one steps forward and Socrates now lists the names of seven men who are there at the trial, any one of whom could step forward and claim, as past associates of the philosopher, that they have been corrupted by his influence.

The defence speech draws to a close with some startling

declarations by Socrates. He will not, he says, beg for mercy or parade his relatives and three children, an adolescent and two smaller boys, before the court in the hope of arousing pity for their plight in the event of his conviction. He feels it is dishonourable for a city like Athens to suggest that virtuous people are cowards and scared of death. He also knows it is ethically wrong to interfere with the due process of law and that that it would be impious of him to act in this way. He thus leaves the jury to decide whether he is guilty. Juries did not discuss the case amongst themselves in any formal sense. Once Socrates had stopped speaking, each cast his vote into one of two urns.

According to Plato, 280 jurors returned a verdict of guilty and 220 a verdict of not guilty. If Socrates did have to contend with the kind of long-held prejudices that he sets out to refute in his defence speech, then perhaps the margin of 60 votes is a surprising one, suggesting that he successfully changed the minds of many Athenians. The 280 who found him guilty had not voted for any particular penalty because none had been fixed by law for this case. The prosecution called for the death penalty, but it was now open to the defendant to propose a counter-penalty and for the jury to decide between the two punishments. Xenophon and Plato give different accounts of what happened next.

According to Xenophon, Socrates suggests no counter-penalty because he feels he is ready to die. He has lived pleasantly, reached a good age and does not relish the prospect of declining into old age and illness. He will not allow his friends to offer a counter-penalty – when they suggest exile, he asks if they know *of any place beyond the borders of Attica where death could not approach him* – and when his friend Apollodorus breaks down and exclaims how it grieves him to see Socrates die so unjustly, he replies *my much-loved Apollodorus! Wouldst thou rather they had condemned me justly?*[146]

Plato has Socrates address the jury a second time and explain that, were he to offer a counter-penalty, a fitting one would be free meals at the Prytaneum. This would be a just recognition of his services to the city and, as with the analogy drawn with Achilles earlier, would establish the practise of philosophy as on a par with martial valour. It seems an odd suggestion on the part of someone whose life is at stake, hardly designed to win over wavering jurors, but Socrates insists that it makes more sense than entertaining sports champions, because the *Olympic victor makes you think yourself happy; I make you happy.*[147]

He rejects alternative penalties like imprisonment or exile, but he is prepared to pay the largest fine he can afford, one mina of silver. This amounted to eight years of wages for a labourer, a considerable sum, and the sum is immediately increased by Socrates' friends, including Plato, who between them raise it to 30 minas.

The jury votes on a penalty and rejects the offer of a fine, sentencing Socrates to death instead. According to Diogenes Laertius, writing some 600 years later, the vote for the death penalty was passed by an even larger majority than the first guilty vote, 360 against 140. If this is true, perhaps some members of the jury were so outraged by Socrates' suggestion of free meals at the Prytaneum as to change their mind about the severity of the punishment he deserved. Diogenes Laertius may not be a reliable source, however, and it is equally likely that some of the jurors, prepared to find him guilty in principle, were not equally committed to seeing him die and would have voted against the death penalty.

Having received the death penalty, Socrates makes a third and final speech to the jury, according to both Plato and Xenophon. Addressing them directly, he says that those who convicted him

The **Prytaneum** was a state building in the agora at Athens where, in a hearth sacred to the goddess Hestia, a symbolic fire was kept burning that represented the heart and home of the city. The Prytaneum included a dining area for distinguished citizens who received free meals at the expense of the *polis* in acknowledgement of their service to the city. Such special citizens included victors at the Olympic Games.

voted the way they did because he was not prepared shamelessly to appeal to their emotions in the manner of other defendants. He has no regrets over his trial defence, saying that death is not something to be avoided at all costs and in his situation he behaved honourably. He prophesies for those who convicted him: *You did this in the belief that you would avoid giving an account of your life, but I maintain that quite the opposite will happen to you.*[148] How the jurors felt about their decision is not known but there is reason to think that Athens later came to regret its treatment of Socrates. Diogenes Laertius says that Meletus was put to death and Anytus and Lycon banished because of their role in prosecuting the philosopher. There is no corroborating evidence to support this, though Xenophon says that Anytus was subsequently held in low regard.

Socrates confronts death with equanimity: it is either a complete *nothing* or a *change and a relocating for the soul*, and if it is a nothingness it will be as welcome a relief as a long dreamless sleep, *for all eternity would then seem to be no more than a single night.*[149] If there is some kind of afterlife, Socrates says mischievously, he looks forward to meeting the souls of others who have been put to death unjustly. There will also be the opportunity to meet luminaries like Homer and Odysseus as well as (and here there is a hint of humour) plenty of time to question and examine people as to their claims to wisdom. He ends on an ironic note, asking his accusers to observe his sons as they grow up, and if they show signs of caring more for money than their souls, *or if they think they are somebody when they are nobody,*[150] to avenge themselves on Socrates by causing as much grief for his sons as he did to them when he was alive, castigating them for not caring for what is really important in life. Plato's *Apology* then draws to an end, with Socrates summing up the situation they have all reached: *the hour to part has come. I go to die, you go to live.*[151] In his very last words, he wonders which of them is facing the better proposition and acknowledges that he does not know. The *Apology* ends, as it began, with a denial of knowledge.[152]

An illustration of the battle between Theseus and the Minotaur

There were no appeal procedures in Athenian law and execution was normally carried out immediately, but it so happened at the time of the trial that the voyage to Delos of a sacred ship was underway and no state executions were allowed until the ship returned, a delay of some 30 days according to Xenophon.

Since the end of the trial Socrates has been held in a prison near the court. When the returning ship is spotted off Sunium, the headland to the southeast of Attica and some 50 kilometres from Athens, there is only one more day left of Socrates' life. This is the news he hears from his old friend Crito and it provides the setting for Plato's *Crito*. Various arguments are made by Crito in an attempt to convince Socrates that he should take the final opportunity to escape prison and seek exile abroad. These arguments are rebuffed. There is no historical evidence to suggest that a conversation of this kind ever took place, but it is possible that an escape was proposed during the period of his imprisonment. There

The voyage of a sacred ship to Delos, an island sacred to Apollo, commemorated the victory of Theseus, an Athenian, over the Minotaur of Crete. The Athenians promised Apollo an annual voyage of celebration to Delos if Theseus returned home safely. This was an ancient festival and it had been revived during the Peloponnesian War as a way of giving thanks to Apollo for the end of the plague.

would have been time to plan it and Crito implies that everything is ready if only Socrates will agree.

Socrates refuses to escape because he would be breaking the terms of an unspoken agreement made between a citizen of Athens and the body politic. He imagines what the Laws of Athens would say to him, pointing out that as a citizen he always had the right to leave Athens and live elsewhere. He chose instead to stay in Athens and accept its laws and he cannot now ignore one of these laws just because he failed to convince the jury. The court that convicted Socrates was a lawful one and as a citizen he is morally bound to accept its verdict. It does not follow that every citizen is bound to blindly obey a law if it involves wrongdoing, as Socrates himself demonstrated when he refused to countenance the motion for the collective trial of the naval commanders after the battle of Arginusae. The obligation to obey the law is also not inconsistent with Socrates' declaration during his trial that were he to be released on the condition that he cease philosophising, he would refuse to do so. Disobedience on moral grounds is permissible if

An engraving of J-L David's painting of the death of Socrates

one is prepared to accept the consequences. In this case, Socrates is prepared to accept the consequences imposed by his city's court and he awaits death calmly.

The final scene of Socrates' life, his death, is immortalised in Plato's *Phaedo*. His wife, Xanthippe, is in the prison cell with their youngest child and Socrates asks Crito to arrange for her to be taken home. He thinks of her again when he prepares to bathe before taking the hemlock. If he does not take a bath, he explains to Crito, the task will be left to the women and he can save them the trouble.

His three children are brought to him for the last time and he says goodbye to them and, always courteous, to the women of his household. His gaoler is reduced to tears as he too says farewell. Socrates calls for the hemlock potion to be prepared and a slave is sent to fetch an assistant, who arrives with the potion and instructions. Socrates offers a prayer to the gods and drinks the poison. As mentioned earlier, Plato's account of a calm and dignified death is quite possibly accurate, but what remains a mystery are the final words spoken by Socrates, *Crito, we owe a cock to Asclepius; make this offering to him and do not forget.*[153] It is probable that these words will remain an enigma – no one has produced an explanation that convinces by virtue of supporting textual or historical evidence – but Nietzsche may have been on the right track when he saw Socrates giving thanks for the imminent 'recovery' from the sickness we call life. In Xenophon, Socrates speaks eloquently of his feelings about approaching death: *Know you not that hitherto I have granted to no man that he hath lived either better, or even more pleasurably than I ... if my life should be still prolonged, it can hardly be but the infirmities of old age will likewise come upon me ... life would not be life but a wearisome burden.*[154] Having lived a long and happy life, he has no regrets about bowing out while still in possession of his faculties, and in a way it is a blessing. Sacrificing a cock to Asclepius would be one way of expressing gratitude for the way things have worked out.

In the Footsteps of Socrates

Socrates' influence on later Greek and Roman philosophy was immense and endured for the whole of this vast period, from the conquests of Alexander the Great, beginning in 334, through the rise of Rome, the expansion of its empire and its collapse in the 5th century AD. Most of the original philosophical texts of the Hellenistic era, 300–150, are lost, but Latin writers translated and quoted from many of them. The schools of philosophy that emerged after Socrates – founded by Plato, Aristotle, Epicurus and Zeno – maintained their influence in the Roman world until Platonism emerged supreme in the 3rd century AD. The first of the Cynics was a follower of Socrates, Antisthenes, and his ideas developed into a movement under Diogenes (c. 400–325) although a school was never founded along the formal lines of Epicureanism under Epicurus and Stoicism under Zeno.

In their highly distinctive ways, the Cynics, Stoics and Epicureans sought wisdom and, following Socrates, battled with ignorance, their own and others'. Most of them did not claim, like the Sophists, to be able to teach goodness as if it were another craft knowledge. They learned from Socrates that right living comes from within the person and so they spoke of the importance of mindfulness, self-control and meditation and many of them tried to live their lives accordingly.[155]

Socrates' concern with philosophical dialogue as a therapeutic method and the importance he attached to *living* philosophically, what might be called his existential imperative, can be traced in all the schools of Hellenistic philosophy. All the schools focus on the importance of making a choice about how to live, adopting a mental state, communing with oneself and living spiritually – not spiritually in the theological sense but in the way Socrates' whole being, his spirit or his soul, bore witness to his art of living. In different ways, this is as obvious in Xenophon as it is in Plato – a Socrates who is eternally asking questions, conversing, listening, clarifying. The Cynics went to an extreme, divorcing themselves as much as possible from the profane world and adopting a primitivist lifestyle that reflected the importance they attached to austere living in conformity with nature. Stoicism developed from Cynicism and emphasised the unimportance of distractions that we cannot control – wealth, fame, possessions and so on – and the importance of our moral nature, something we can exercise freely and consciously by ourselves. Stoicism traced its own genealogy in a direct line from Socrates, through the Cynics Antisthenes and Diogenes and on to Zeno who is said to have founded Stoicism after reading Xenophon's *Memoirs*.

The Stoic Seneca wrote how Socrates responded to a man who was complaining to him that he found no fulfillment in travel: 'Why are you surprised that travel does you no good? You always take yourself with you.' Seneca also noted how Socrates was said to have responded to a slap in the face: 'It's a nuisance not knowing when to go out wearing a helmet.'[156]

Epicureanism, despite what the word has come to mean, was also concerned with the moral basis of happiness, the consequent importance of avoiding those desires that only cause worry and the spiritual value of living mindfully and taking care of one's soul. It was Socrates, questioning how we live, who first brought what would be the concerns of Stoics and Epicureans into the open.

Early Christian writers found in Socrates what they wanted to find and turned the pagan philosopher into a proto-Christian.

Medieval scholars were initially more interested in the later Plato before turning to Aristotle, so that Socrates remained in the background. It is Montaigne in the 16th century who re-discovers the radical Socrates and finds inspiration in the Greek philosopher's programme for self-examination, self-knowledge and self-creation.[157]

The impact of Socrates on modern thought arises from his insistence that what you know is less important than how and why you come to know something – and what you know is less valuable than what you do with what you know.

'I recognised that the surest thing was to entrust myself and my need to myself; and that if it happened that I was lodged only coolly in fortune's favours I should recommend myself all the more strongly to my own favour, and attach myself and look all the more closely to myself ... Everyone rushes elsewhere and into the future, because no one has arrived at himself.'

Montaigne, *The Essays*.[158]

In the course of Socrates' conversations, and this comes across as clearly in Xenophon as in Plato, it becomes obvious that many of the Athenians merely parrot conventional ideas when asked about their values and ethics. They mouth general opinions but, when questioned, cannot explain their reasons for holding them or how they relate to other values that they claim to believe in. Socrates is not advocating a new set of values, but by exposing the lack of thought behind many people's convictions, he is more radical than many a revolutionary. If people lack reasoned convictions and live on the basis of conventional morality, their lack of knowledge could actually become a dangerous form of ignorance. It could expose them to the fashions of public opinion, manipulation by vested interests and the menace of crowd psychology. This is what seems to have happened when Athenians wanted to prosecute and execute the generals for their failure to pick up the survivors after the battle of Arginusae, and something like it happened again when, in the stress of post-war defeat, Athens made Socrates a scapegoat for its fears and uncertainties.

Socrates did not possess the kind of knowledge that might ideally underpin ethics and morality, but he knew the value of trying to obtain it and the value of assisting others to reach a point where they too could see the need to look to themselves for the foundations of their values. For Socrates, the Delphic injunction to 'know thyself' was a strategy that would not lead to revelation and certainty but to a critical self-examination that would result in a reasoned direction of the will and a change of conduct. There was no body of ethical knowledge that could be guaranteed and, as is clear from Socrates' mystical divine sign and his meditative states of concentration, a linear rationality could not by itself open the way to such knowledge, but personal commitment enabled Socrates to lead a good life and the possibility was open for others to do the same.

This was the Socrates who so deeply impressed and influenced Kierkegaard – 'O Socrates … Your adventure was the same as mine'[159] – a philosopher whose ideas are sketched in the early chapters of most histories of existentialism. Kierkegaard, like Socrates, was struck by many people's preference not to know themselves. He was also like Socrates in stressing the need for each person to become aware of their unreflective thinking

Søren Kierkegaard (1813–55) was born into a wealthy family in Copenhagen. A powerful religious experience affected him as a young man and he abandoned a life of idle self-indulgence, dedicated himself to serious study and planned to become a pastor. In 1840 he became engaged to Regine Olsen but broke off the engagement less than a year later. He remained a bachelor and began publishing philosophical works under a series of pseudonyms. He remained a believer in Christianity but attacked the Church in Denmark relentlessly and on his deathbed refused to receive the Eucharist.

and look to themselves for their values and hence the choices they make in life, not relying on public opinion or convention to guide them. An absolute commitment to a set of values, freely chosen, was the only authentic way to live for Kierkegaard. He came to see that this involved more than just rational decision-making. In order to draw a distinction between the intellectual awareness of a 'truth' and the self-commitment that comes from a personal experience that changes one's whole understanding of life, he stressed the need for what he called 'subjective truth'.

Kierkegaard's notion of subjective truth is not the same as the idea that a set of beliefs are true simply because someone firmly believes them to be so. It is not enough merely to think of oneself as having certain moral values, for this kind of objective understanding does not necessarily find authentic expression in the way one lives. It is through an individual's personal existence, a 'state of becoming', that the truth is lived, not as a theory or a set of concepts, but as an inward experience. This is a personal account we hold with ourselves, so that only I can really know the truth of my existence: 'subjectivity, inwardness, is truth ... the inwardness of the existing person is the truth'.[160] This does not mean that the truth is something that resides only inside our heads, but rather that its authenticity arises from a deep sense of living our lives in accordance with ethical values that determine our conduct and our sense of who we are. Such values can be rationally defended, but it is only when they are experienced as a way of being that they become worthwhile.

Kierkegaard extolled Socrates because he saw him as a kindred spirit who, in his own way, made the same important distinction between subjective truth, as something profoundly lived, and 'objective' knowledge as a mere state of intellectual awareness. When Socrates speaks of caring for one's soul, the *psuchē*, the spirit of a person that is bound up with their will, desire and consciousness, Kierkegaard sees this in terms of attending to the need for subjective truth. For both philosophers, the commitment to a set of moral ideals was authenticated in the activities of our lives, and the source came from the depths of the self. Like Socrates, Kierkegaard does not set out to teach a body of knowledge and in his writings he adopts instead a series of pseudonyms and authorial voices, sometimes contradictory ones, so that one cannot easily and conveniently pigeon-hole his ideas and, having grasped them intellectually, be spared the task of taking them subjectively on board and changing one's state of consciousness and way of being. 'Socrates was a teacher of the ethical, but he was aware that there is no direct relation between the teacher and the learner, because inwardness is truth, and inwardness in the two is precisely the path away from each other.'[161] A traditional teacher, like a Sophist, can only present truth in an objective manner, as something to be learned empirically, but a teacher of Socrates' kind wants truth to be inwardly experienced and discovered by the learner so that they become a different kind of person.

Morality becomes objective when it is codified into a set of rules to which we are happy to subscribe because they create an illusionary comfort. This is what Socrates discovered when, inspired by Delphi's oracle, he questioned people who were knowledgeable in an objective way and who mistakenly assumed that this enabled them to make ethical judgements. Kierkegaard found just such people around him in Copenhagen and realised they objectified their Christian beliefs in a way that conveniently allowed them to become hypocrites. Socrates tried to help people realise the inadequacy of an objective approach to ethics, but he could only do this by leading them to a state of confusion and hoping that they would respond to it with self-examination, out of which subjective truth might emerge. Both philosophers want to show how concepts like justice or responsibility elude language in the insistence that they must be lived and not just acquired intellectually.

An existentialist state of being defined the nature of life

for both Kierkegaard and Socrates. It is a short conceptual step from an awareness of Socratic ignorance to the frightening prospect of living in a world devoid of objective truths. In such circumstances, conventional morality, far from being a signpost in life's journey, obscures the need to find one's own way and accept being alone with one's freedom. The search for subjective truth becomes the individual's lonely responsibility. Kierkegaard spoke of this existential awareness as a state of absurdity, because it is ultimately beyond rational understanding and relies on a leap of faith.

While Kierkegaard's theistic existentialism is based on accepting our absolute dependence on God, Socrates' existentialism takes an atheistic form and bases its authenticity on a different kind of faith, a trust in the goodness of human nature. Both philosophers share a belief in a foundation for ethics that is not fully explicable in terms of rational argument. Socrates always sought a rational basis for investigations of an ethical kind – for what other basis would allow for a possibly therapeutic inquiry when communicating with others? – hoping to arrive at ethical knowledge that was as secure as the craft knowledge of tanners or horse trainers. He never found such a basis, perhaps coming to know that it could not exist, but pursued it as the best possible way of communicating with himself and others. Kierkegaard inherited from him this vision of a world in which we must commit ourselves to, have faith in, a set of values that have no rational certainty.

Kierkegaard has nothing but praise for Socrates and looks to him as a model to emulate. Nietzsche, the other great philosopher of the 19th century who engages with Socrates, finds it far more complicated to explain how he relates to him, a reflection of the complications within his own thought. In *The Birth of Tragedy*, published in 1872, he identifies Socrates as the enemy of the spirit of Greek tragedy. Nietzsche expressed his admiration for the tragedies of Aeschylus and Sophocles in terms of what he called the Apollonian and the Dionysian. Apollo, the god whose oracle at Delphi played such an important role in Socrates' life, becomes for Nietzsche the face of rationality, individual form and moderation, while Dionysus stands for mysticism, communalism and excess. Such distinct attributes for the two gods existed in antiquity but Nietzsche turns them into an oppositional pair for his own philosophical purposes, using them to distinguish different sets of attitudes and responses towards the nature of existence. Classical Greek tragedy, argues Nietzsche, fuses the Apollonian and the Dionysian in a celebration of the human endeavour to heroically rise above a meaningless universe while at the same time accepting the inevitability of failure in any such attempt. Left to their own dynamics, the Apollonian would descend into the vulgar militarism of ancient Rome and the Dionysian would sink into a resigned passivity, but working together they produce a unique art form that metaphysically venerates human worth despite the indifference of a world that denies any rational significance to our action.

Friedrich Nietzsche, born in 1844, was just 24 years old when appointed professor of classical philology at the University of Basel. His first book, *The Birth of Tragedy*, was greeted with scorn and hostility. By 1889, when he suffered a mental breakdown from which he never recovered, he had produced over a dozen books. He died in 1900. Nietzsche's impact on modern thought continues to be profound and he remains one of the greatest, if most controversial, of all philosophers.

Nietzsche claims that Socrates killed Greek tragedy by introducing a spirit of rationality. This spirit finds expression in the plays of Euripides – according to Diogenes Laertius, Socrates and Euripides were on close terms and Nietzsche builds on this supposed relationship[162] – and it undermines the life-sustaining insights of traditional Attic tragedy. By placing reason above instinct, morality is able to impose itself on the world and dogmatism is allowed to thwart our aspirations. In 'The Problem of Socrates', one of the essays in *Twilight of the Idols*, published in 1888, Nietzsche offers an explanation for Socrates' influence in antiquity. His unhealthy achievement was to introduce an intellectual dimension into the Greek love of competition, transforming reason into a tyrant that promises to master the instincts. The need to fight and control instinct, however, is essentially a symptom of decadence for Nietzsche because it prioritises one impulse, reason, at the expense of accommodating all the instincts. By ironing out the multitude of impulses that go to make up a healthy individual and a healthy society, Socrates taught a distrust of instincts and capacities instead of finding a way of integrating them into the self. The result is a wearisome antipathy to life so that living becomes an illness, something that requires justification in the form of reason.

Nietzsche sees Socrates' legacy as a falling away from the older and more healthy Greek way of being that simply accepted life, its joys and its horrors, and expressed itself artistically in the dramas of classical tragedy. For Nietzsche, what made the older Greek culture so magnificent was its ability to live without the need for some comforting rationale, some fig leaf of supposed understanding that would offer an explanation for why there is something rather than nothing. The Greeks had learned to live with the irrational, not by becoming irrational but by expending a great deal of effort in creating a code for living that allowed them to affirm and love existence without the need for conscious explanation. Socrates elevates reason and by teaching

'Who is this man [Socrates] who single-handedly dares negate the Greek character, which in the form of Homer, Pindar, and Aeschylus, of Phidias, Pericles, Pythia, and Dionysus, as the deepest abyss and the highest peak is assured of our astonished adoration? What daemonic power is this which dares to spill this magic potion in the dust? What demigod is this, to whom the ghostly chorus of the noblest of humanity must shout: "Woe! Woe! Your powerful fist has destroyed the beautiful world; it collapses, it falls apart!"'

Nietzsche, *The Birth of Tragedy*.[163]

The German philosopher Friedrich Nietzsche photographed in 1885

us to distrust instinct as a mark of original sin creates Christiani-ty's prototype.

If Nietzsche's engagement with Socrates was as single-mindedly negative as this there would be little cause to trace Nietzsche in his footsteps. But reading Nietzsche always involves grappling with marvellous and ambiguous profundities that come wrapped up in hyperbole and generalisations, and his relationship with Socrates is a love-hate one that produces as many questions as it does answers. Nietzsche's ideal of happiness, embracing life by etching a style of living for oneself as an individual, is an existentialist one. It rejects any form of dogmatism in favour of what he calls perspectivism, part of which entails living with multiple interpretations of the world. Given Nietzsche's anarchist project of self-realisation, why does he appear so blind to the similarities between himself and Socrates?[164] Nor did Socrates rely solely on reason when it came to the conduct of his own life: his mystical divine sign was also his guide to action, and although he searched for knowledge of moral excellence he never found it. Yet this seems to cut no ice with Nietzsche and the divine sign of Socrates is condemned by him because it always expressed itself as a negative, a curb on his instincts. Why did Nietzsche attribute a dogmatism to Socrates that could have been laid at the door of Plato? Instead, Socrates is suspected of being responsible for corrupting Plato: 'To be sure, to speak of spirit and the good as Plato did meant standing truth on her head and denying *perspective* itself, the basic condition of all life; indeed, one may ask as a physician: "how could such a malady attack this loveliest product of antiquity, Plato? Did the wicked Socrates corrupt him after all? And have deserved his hemlock?"'[165]

Nietzsche also admits, however: 'Socrates, to confess it simply, stands so close to me, that I am almost always fighting a battle with him.'[166] Although Nietzsche criticizes Socrates vehemently he also, at other times, praises him for his tremendous individuality and the instinctive force of his commitment to rational argument: 'On the other hand, however, the logical drive which emerged in Socrates was utterly forbidden to turn against itself; in this boundless torrent it demonstrated a power of nature such as we encounter to our horrified surprise only in the greatest instinctive forces.'[167] Reason and instinct, normally diametrically opposed forces in Nietzsche, are here conjoined so that reason becomes one more facet of our instinctive nature. In trying to puzzle out why Nietzsche can so vindictively attack Socrates while also praising him, the possibility arises that perhaps Nietzsche is uncomfortably aware of similarities between his radicalism and that of Socrates. After all, the problem of the place of reason is faced by him as well. Nietzsche is no irrationalist and in his own highly individual way is setting out to explain himself and offer reasons for why perspectivism is the best basis for living in the world, while also condemning reason as a tool of those who are scared of life and its challenges.

Nietzsche explains human behaviour in terms of a desire for power, an unstoppable push towards self-realisation and a widening of horizons. This is often expressed in the vocabulary of the battlefield, perhaps partly because Nietzsche wants readers to acknowledge the shocking implications of what he is saying, and because of this, the will to power can be misinterpreted as some kind of justification for the crude brutality of the bully or the imperial self-aggrandizement of a superpower state. Nietzsche's highest and warmest praise for those who dare to will to power is expressed in terms of strength of character, resolve of the will and the courageous readiness to overcome oneself. In *Twilight of the Idols*, this is how he characterises Socrates when he retells the story of Socrates agreeing with the physiognomist Zopyrus when he read signs in his face of vice and lust.

'When that physiognomist [Zopyrus] had revealed to Socrates what he was, a cave of every evil lust, the great ironist uttered a phrase that provides the key to him. "That is true,' he said, 'but I have become master of them all." *How* did Socrates become master of himself?'

Nietzsche, *Twilight of the Idols*.[168]

The ambivalence of Nietzsche's attitude towards Socrates runs through his work, a jagged but recurring pattern. *Twilight of the Idols* is one of his last works but in the conclusion to his analysis of Socrates in *The Birth of Tragedy*, his very first book, Nietzsche credits him with an influence that actually guarantees the continuing possibility of art. In a complex account that qualifies his earlier condemnation, Nietzsche realises that Socrates is 'the single point around which so-called world history turns and twists'.[169]

If it were not for the revolution in thought that Socrates represents, if reason and logic were not elevated in the way they were, science would never have progressed. A possible alternative course for world history is envisaged in apocalyptic terms as a 'horrible ethic of genocide from compassion'.[170]

Socrates, now a world-saving optimist because of his eternal belief in the search for knowledge, inaugurates a new kind of Greek wisdom, and Nietzsche admits to feeling the powerful charm of a way of thinking that offers the prospect of making existence intelligible. Such a prospect, however, always remains a delusion for Nietzsche because there is a natural limit to the optimism that the edifice of reason is built on and any noble enquirer after truth will eventually realise this. At such a pivotal

'For if one were to imagine the whole incalculable sum of energy which has been consumed by this world tendency [Socratic rationalism], employed *not* in the service of knowledge but instead to the practical, that is, egoistic ends of individuals and peoples, then the instinctive pleasure in life would probably have been so weakened in widespread struggles of annihilation and ongoing emigrations that, with suicide having become habitual, the individual would perhaps feel driven to strangle his parents and friends by the last vestige of a sense of duty towards them ... a pessimism which moreover exists and has existed everywhere in the world, where art in some form or other, particularly as religion and science, has not appeared as a remedy and defence against that miasma.'

Nietzsche, *The Birth of Tragedy*.[171]

moment, expressed by Nietzsche in the image of logic as a snake that so coils around itself as to bite its own tail, a new kind of understanding may emerge, a knowledge tragically aware of its inherent limitations and in dire need of art as a remedy. From this point of view, Socrates is vindicated and becomes a maker of Dionysian music. This is the Socrates that Nietzsche praises in *Human, All Too Human*, published six years after *The Birth of Tragedy*, as someone who was both wise and frivolous – a rare combination that he accords only to great thinkers. This is the Socrates who delights in dancing portrayed in Xenophon's *Memoirs*,[172] the book that he speculates could one day replace the Bible as a worthy guide to good living. In *Human, All Too Human*, Socrates is lauded as the greatest philosopher, the ideal iconoclast who is described, not as a gadfly, but a vivisectionist who cuts into conventional thought and lays bare its hollowness. Socrates is one of those rare individuals who dares to say, 'We have to go thither, out yonder, where *you* today are least at home'.[173]

To follow someone who is leading 'out yonder', perhaps to uncharted territory, to a place where one does not feel comfortably at home, is not easy. Kierkegaard and Nietzsche, in their own ways and for their own reasons, accepted such a challenge. They followed in the footsteps of Socrates in the sense that they looked into themselves, asked difficult questions and examined life. In their own ways they came to see that Socrates was right when he said that we do not understand ourselves well enough and that *the most important thing is not life but the good life*.[174] In his trial, according to Plato, Socrates reminded his jury of how Achilles behaved when he faced a choice between doing what he felt was right, avenging the death of his friend Patroclus, and doing what would ensure a longer life for himself, by not returning to the battlefield at Troy. Achilles had no hesitation in making his decision. In prison, waiting for the return of the ship from Delos that would signify the time for his execution, Socrates was equally unhesitant in choosing to do what he thought right even if it cost him his life: *I am the kind of man who listens to nothing within me but the argument that on reflection seems best to me. I cannot, now that this fate has come upon me, discard the arguments I used; they seem to me much the same. I value and respect the same principles as before, and if we have no better arguments to bring up at this moment, be sure that I shall not agree with you, not even if the power of the majority were to frighten us with more bogeys, as if we were children, with threats of incarcerations and executions and confiscation of property.*[175] Achilles, though, dies with public honour and is recognised as the greatest of warriors by his comrades; Socrates died with public dishonour, rejected by his fellow citizens. In this respect, he was more like Ajax who, after Achilles, was the bravest of the warriors at Troy and therefore the one with the most just claim to inherit the armour of Achilles. Socrates himself draws the comparison in his final speech to the jury, after he has been condemned to death, when he envisages meeting in Hades great men of the past: *It would be a wonderful way for me to spend my time whenever I met Palamedes and Ajax, the son of Telamon, and any other of the men of old who died through an unjust conviction.*[176]

In an important sense, no one follows in the footsteps of Socrates because he did not lay down a path so that others could follow him and reach the same destination. Kierkegaard understood this and he found his own way, guided only by the spirit of Socrates. Nietzsche writes of Socrates daring us to make a journey where we will be alone, unguided and uncomforted, but does not make the mistake of thinking he also provided signposts indicating what direction to take when a crossroads is reached. Socrates provides a starting point and a moral compass but no more. A similar kind

Ajax, son of Telamon, was a great warrior who died a tragic death. At Troy he battled bravely for the Greeks and engaged in single combat with the Trojan hero Hector. In Homer, Ajax is slow-spoken but magnificently brave, leading many an attack on the Trojans and always reliable in covering tactical retreats of the Greek forces. He contrasts dramatically with the wily Odysseus with whom he loses a wrestling match even though he was the stronger man. After the death of Achilles, there is a dispute between Ajax and Odysseus over who has the best claim to the armour of the slain warrior. The armour is awarded to Odysseus and Ajax is driven by anger and his sense of honour to commit suicide.

of guidance was offered by someone who died around the same time that Socrates was born. The Buddha, Siddharta Gautama, also held the view that each person had to find for themselves the truth that was exemplified in the Buddha's own life. Like Socrates, he engaged in dialogue but wrote nothing, founded no school, appointed no successors. He spoke of four noble truths: that life is suffering, that the cause of suffering is desire, that when this craving is eradicated suffering will cease and that following the eight-fold guide to behaviour will lead to the eradication of desire. The eight-fold steps are: right view, right intention, right speech, right action, right livelihood, right effort, right mindfulness and right concentration.

The Buddha shares with Socrates the wish to influence how people conduct their lives and he too offers a therapeutic approach, eschewing a concern with ontology or theology in favour of the ethical. For Socrates, virtue was happiness and the source of virtue lay with the individual's commitment to an examination of their life. Ignorance led people astray so that, for example, wealth and possessions were mistakenly seen as a way of finding happiness. The Buddha said something similar, seeing unhappiness as rooted in an ignorance that led people to attach undue importance to impermanent things: 'Being united with what is not liked is suffering, separation from what is liked is suffering, not to get what one wants is suffering.'[177] *Karma* was the choice that each person makes and the Buddha brings the same existential quality to his philosophy as Socrates. It is up to the individual to find a way of living virtuously, managing one's emotions and practising the kind of moral self-discipline that Xenophon finds so admirable in Socrates.

Such a life, for the Buddha, was necessary in order to achieve the last of the eight-fold steps, right concentration, that made possible the state of meditation that held out the promise of an enduring equanimity. It is impossible to say for sure what was the

nature of the meditative state that Alcibiades observed Socrates
achieving when they were on military duty in the north Aegean
together, but it bears some resemblance to the Buddha's medita-
tions. There is also a similarity between the end of the Buddha's
life and Socrates' final hours. Both men lived long lives for the
times in which they lived – the Buddha was around eighty, ten
years older than Socrates – and they both approached death with
calmness and fortitude. The Buddha's attendant, Ananda, was as
upset by the Buddha's death as Crito was by Socrates', and like
Socrates' old friend he has to be comforted and made to realise that
death is not something to be feared and avoided at all costs.[178]

To see the influence of Socrates on Kierkegaard and Nietzsche
and to compare him with the Buddha could leave the false impression that he was essentially a thinker for the private individual,
concerned only with the inner nature of the self and its redemp-
tion. The Buddha, Kierkegaard and Nietzsche were all adversarial
figures, deeply at odds with the world around them and profoundly
critical of conventional thought. Far from being apolitical, they
sought to influence how people behaved in society by concerning
themselves with the nature of existence and the values by which
we live. The same attitude forced Socrates into conscious conflict
with the state on more than occasion and his non-conformity led
eventually to his death: it is difficult to know what is more political
than this. Socrates' philosophical conversation in prison with Crito
examines the relationship between the ethical individual and the
society to which they belong. In 1942, the French sociologist and
philosopher Georges Friedman also dwelt on the relationship and
offered a possible mediation between the two in a way with which
Socrates might have concurred:

'Take flight each day! At least for a moment, however brief,
as long as it is intense. Every day a "spiritual exercise", alone or
in the company of a man who also wishes to better himself ...
Leave ordinary time behind. Make an effort to rid yourself of your

own passions ... become eternal by surpassing yourself. This inner effort is necessary, this ambition, just. Many are those who are entirely absorbed in militant politics, in the preparation for the social revolution. Rare, very rare, are those who, in order to prepare for the revolution, wish to become worthy of it.'[179]

Or, to put it like Socrates, *the unexamined life is not worth living*.[180]

Notes

1. All dates, unless stated as AD, are BC.
2. Plato, *Phaedo*, 118a. Unless otherwise stated, quotations from Plato are taken from *Plato: Complete Works*, edited by John M Cooper (Hackett, Indianapolis: 1997).
3. Thomas C Brickhouse and Nicholas D Smith, *Plato and the Trial of Socrates* (Routledge, New York and London: 2004) pp 258–64.
4. Brickhouse and Smith, *Plato and the Trial of Socrates,* p 265.
5. In this regard, Xenophon's *Memoirs of Socrates* includes homely advice on eating well and manners at the dinner table (3.13–14), reflections on the functional beauty of the human face (1.4), and tales of talking animals justifying work relationships (2.7). From Ashley, Spelman, Smith and Fielding, *The Complete Works of Xenophon* (London, Chatto and Windus: 1875).
6. This is the view of Gregory Vlastos, *Socrates: Ironist and Moral Philosopher* (Cambridge University Press, Cambridge: 1991), W K C Guthrie, *Socrates* (Cambridge University Press, Cambridge: 1971) ch 1, and C C W Taylor, *Socrates* (OUP, Oxford: 1998) ch 3. Alexander Nehamas, *The Art of Living* (Cambridge University Press, Cambridge: 1998) agrees, though his arrangement of Plato's early and middle texts is a little different and he sees the *Gorgias* and the *Meno* as introducing a new stage in Plato's thought.

Socrates appears in all of Plato's dialogues, except the *Laws*, but in the middle and later texts – including *Republic* (except Book 1), *Phaedrus*, *Cratylus* and *Philebus* – he becomes less of an individual and more a general figure representing a philosophical voice. In two late works, the *Sophist* and the *Statesman*, the presence of Socrates is very marginal.

7. Aristotle, *Metaphysics,* 1.6.987 B I, in John Ferguson, *Socrates: A Source Book* (Macmillan, London: 1970) p 181.

8. Aristotle, *Metaphysics,* 13.4.1078 B 17–32, in Ferguson, *Socrates,* p 181.

9. Most of these sources for Socrates are collected in Ferguson, *Socrates*.

10. Aristotle, *Logical Works*, 30.953 A 10 and 27, in Ferguson, *Socrates*, p 181.

11. W K C Guthrie, *Socrates*, p 77 and Ferguson, *Socrates*, pp 192–3.

12. Plato, *Symposium*, 220c–d.

13. Plato, *Symposium*, 21e.

14. Plato, *Symposium*, 221e–222a.

15. Plato, *Apology*, 31d.

16. Nietzsche, when he wanted to ridicule Socrates as a high-minded and interfering moralist, suggested the divine sign was probably only an ear infection.

17. Søren Kierkegaard, *The Concept of Irony with Continual Reference to Socrates* (Princeton University Press, Princeton: 1989) p 12.

18. Kierkegaard, *The Concept of Irony*, p 269.

19. Aeschylus, *Prometheus and Other Plays* (Penguin, London: 1966) p 127.

20. Quoted in Robin Barrow, *Athenian Democracy* (Macmillan Education, London: 1973, repr 1978) pp 20–1.

21. Quoted in Barrow, *Athenian Democracy*, p 38.

22. Thucydides, *The Peloponnesian War*, Book 2, ch 4 (Penguin, London: 1964).

23. Plato, *Apology*, 17d; and *Crito*, 52e.

24. Plato, *Euthyphro, 11b*, and *Alcibiades,* 121a.

25. Plato*, Laches* 181a and *Crito,* 50e.

26. Plato, *Theaetetus*, 150c.

27. Xenophon, *Banquet* 2 from *The Complete Works of Xenophon*, p 605.

28. Xenophon, *Memoirs of Socrates* 2.2 from *The Complete Works of Xenophon*, p 544.

29. Shakespeare, *The Taming of the Shrew*, Act 1, Scene 2; Henry Fielding, *Tom Jones*, Book 8, chapter xi. In James Joyce, *Ulysses*, chapter 9, lines 232–9, Stephen Dedalus is arguing that Ann Hathaway had a vital impact on Shakespeare and when told that she was a shrew, a mistake in the bard's life, Stephen replies that a genius makes no mistakes, for his errors are 'the portals of discovery'. Asked what useful discovery did Socrates learn from Xanthippe: '— Dialectic, Stephen answered: and from his mother how to bring thoughts into the world.'

30. See, for example, Ferguson, *Socrates*, p 227, with a passage from Plutarch to this effect. Joyce, in the passage from *Ulysses* just referred to, also has Stephen Dedalus speak of Myrto, obliquely referring to the fact that the word Myrto was the ancient Greek equivalent of 'cunt'. See R J Schork, *Greek and Hellenic Culture in Joyce* (University Press of Florida, Gainesville: 1998) p 222.

31. Diogenes Laertius, 'Life of Socrates' from *The Lives and Views of Eminent Philosophers*, in Ferguson, *Socrates*, p 26.

32. Diogenes Laertius, 'Life of Socrates' in Ferguson, *Socrates*, p 26.

33. Ferguson, *Socrates*, p 241 and p 22 and A E Taylor, *Socrates*, p 39 (Peter Davies Limited, London: 1932). Robert Payne,

The Splendour of Greece (Pan Books, London: 1973) pp 139–40, thought it was a statue carved by Socrates that Flaubert found and fondled ecstatically in 1850.

34. Plato, *Phaedo*, 96a.

35. Thucydides, *The Peloponnesian War*, Book 2, ch 4.

36. Plato, *Crito*, 52b.

37. A E Taylor, *Socrates*, pp 65–6.

38. Plato, *Phaedo*, 99e.

39. Xenophon, *Memoirs of Socrates,* from *The Complete Works of Xenophon*, p 521.

40. Xenophon, *Memoirs of Socrates,* from *The Complete Works of Xenophon*, p 597.

41. Paul Cartledge, 'War and Peace' in Paul Cartledge (ed), *The Cambridge Illustrated History of Ancient Greece* (Cambridge University Press, Cambridge:1998) pp 168–9.

42. Thucydides, *The Peloponnesian War*, Book 2, ch 7.

43. Plato, *Symposium*, 220c.

44. Plato, *Symposium*, 220e. Saving the armour was important to avoid the risk of being accused of cowardice on the battlefield, abandoning one's shield and spear.

45. Thucydides, *The Peloponnesian War*, Book 2, ch 5.

46. Thucydides, *The Peloponnesian War*, Book 3, ch 3.

47. Plato, *Laches*, 181b.

48. Plato, *Symposium*, 221c.

49. Thucydides, *The Peloponnesian War*, Book 5, ch 1 and ch 2.

50. Aristophanes, *Peace*, lines 571–9, from Aristophanes, *Plays: 1* (OUP, Oxford: 1970) p 243.

51. Aristophanes, *Clouds*, lines 103 and 362; and lines from a lost play by Ameipsias, in Ferguson, *Socrates*, p 173.

52. Plato, *Symposium*, 215b.

53. Xenophon, *Banquet*, 5, from *The Complete Works of Xenophon*, p 615, and in Ferguson, *Socrates,* p 158.

54. Xenophon, *Banquet*, 5, from *The Complete Works of Xenophon*, p 616, and in Ferguson, *Socrates,* p 159.

55. Quoted in Pierre Hadot, *Philosophy as a Way of Life* (Blackwell, Oxford: 1995) p 148.

56. Plato, *Charmides*, 154c and 155d.

57. Plato, *Symposium*, 218c.

58. Plato, *Symposium*, 219c–d.

59. Plato, *Symposium*, 220a.

60. Plato, *Symposium*, 223d.

61. Plato, *Apology*, 32b–c.

62. Plato, *Apology*, 32c.

63. Thucydides, *The Peloponnesian War*, Book 5, ch 7 and Book 6, ch 1.

64. Plutarch, *Plutarch's Lives*, 'Life of Nicias', translated by Langhorne (Frederick Warne and Co, Vol 1, London: 1884) p 203.

65. Thucydides, *The Peloponnesian War*, Book 7, ch 7.

66. Aristophanes, *Frogs*, line 1425, in Aristophanes, *Plays: 2* (OUP, Oxford: 1970) p 235.

67. Xenophon, *The Affairs of Greece*, 2.2, from *The Complete Works of Xenophon*, p 378.

68. Xenophon, *Hellenica*, 2.2.3 from *The Complete Works of Xenophon*, p 379.

69. Plato, *Apology*, 32d.

70. *Apology*, 32e. Xenophon, *Affairs of Greece,* 1.7, also relates the history of the trial and Socrates' insistence that he will not be party to an illegal act. In Xenophon's *Memoirs of Socrates*, 1.2, there is an account of an earlier exchange between Critias and Socrates.

71. Ferguson, *Socrates*, p 177.

72. The best-known account of this conspiracy theory is be found in I F Stone, *The Trial of Socrates* (Pimlico, London: 1997), first published in 1988.

73. Xenophon, *Defence of Socrates*, from *The Complete Works of Xenophon*, p 515 and in Ferguson, *Socrates*, p 143. Xenophon adds how the son of Anytus did indeed adopt a disreputable lifestyle, 'whereby he became perfectly useless to his country, to his friends and even to himself'.

74. Xenophon, *Memoirs,* 1.2, from *The Complete Works of Xenophon*, p 523 and in Ferguson, *Socrates,* p 148.

75. Plato, *Apology*, 28b.

76. Plato, *Apology*, 29d.

77. For Socrates' approval of the government of Sparta, see Plato's *Apology*, 53a.

78. Plato, *Crito*, 47d.

79. Plato, *Apology*, 18b.

80. Plato, *Apology*, 19b.

81. Plato, *Protagoras*, 313d.

82. Thucydides, *The Peloponnesian War*, Book 6, ch 2.

83. Thucydides, *The Peloponnesian War*, Book 6, ch 8.

84. Plato, *Apology*, 33a.

85. Plato, *Apology*, 19e.

86. Plato, *Apology*, 33b.

87. Plato, *Apology*, 18d.

88. Aristophanes, *Clouds*, line 1509, in Aristophanes, *Plays: 1*, p 163.

89. Aristophanes, *Clouds*, lines 95–100, in Aristophanes, *Plays: 1*, p 163.

90. A de Lamartine, *Homer and Socrates* (J B Lippincott and Co, Philadelphia: 1872) p 64. Quoted in James A Colaiaco, *Socrates Against Athens* (Routledge, London: 2001) p 44.

91. Plato, *Apology*, 23a.

92. Plato, *Apology*, 23c.

93. Plato, *Apology*, 33a.

94. Plato, *Symposium*, 175d.

95. Herodotus tells the story of how Croesus consulted the oracle at Delphi over the wisdom or otherwise of attacking the Persians and was told that if he did then a great empire would fall. Croesus assumed that the *pythia* was referring to the Persian empire and cheerfully launched his attack, only to fail disastrously and belatedly realise that the empire in question was his own. Before consulting the oracle, Croesus had tested its power by sending a messenger there to ask what he was doing exactly 100 days after the messenger had left on his journey. The *pythia* correctly answered that he was cooking a lamb and a tortoise in a bronze pot. Herodotus, *The Histories*, Book 1.

96. Plato, *Apology*, 21b.

97. Plato, *Apology*, 21c.

98. Plato, *Apology*, 22a.

99. Plato, *Apology*, 23b and Lucian, *Hermotimus*, 48, in Ferguson, *Socrates*, p 232.

100. Quoted in G S Kirk, J E Raven and M Schofield, *The Presocratic Philosophers: A Critical History with a Selection of Texts* (Cambridge University Press, Cambridge: 1979) p 123.

101. Plato, *Apology*, 23b.

102. Nietzsche, *Human, All Too Human, A Book for Free Spirits*, §86, vol 2, quoted in Pierre Hadot, *Philosophy as a Way of Life*, p 167. Nietzsche is also quoted by Hadot, p 177, describing Xenophon's *Memoirs* as 'the most attractive book in Greek literature'.

103. Xenophon, *Memoirs*, 1.1.

104. Plato, *Apology*, 22d.

105. Aristotle, *Sophisticated Refutations*, 34.183 B 8, in Ferguson, *Socrates*, p 181.

106. Plato, *Euthyphro*, 7a.

107. Plato, *Euthyphro*, 10a.

108. Plato, *Euthyphro*, 9e–10a.

109. Plato, *Meno*, 97e.

110. Plato, *Euthyphro*, 11c.

111. Plato, *Euthyphro*, 11e.

112. Plato, *Euthyphro*, 15e

113. Plato, *Apology*, 33b.

114. Xenophon, *Memoirs*, 4.4, from *The Complete Works of Xenophon*, p 590.

115. Plato, *Apology*, 36c, in Hadot, *Philosophy as a Way of Life*, p 155; Hadot's translation of Plato here seems more telling than most (see pp vi–vii for the comments of Hadot's own translator).

116. Xenophon, *Memoirs, 4.2,* from *The Complete Works of Xenophon*, p 587.

117. Plato, *Theaetetus*, 149a.

118. Plato, *Symposium*, 221d.

119. Plato, *Laches*, 177e.

120. Plato, *Theaetetus*, 150d.

121. Plato, *Meno*, 80a.

122. 'The Lake Isle of Innisfree', W B Yeats, *The Poems* (J M Dent & Sons, Everyman's Library, London: 1992) p 60. Nietzsche, *Beyond Good and Evil*, 12 (Penguin, London: 2003) p 43.

123. Plato, *Alcibiades*, 130e.

124. Plato, *Protagoras*, 314b.

125. Plato, *Apology*, 31e.

126. *Apology*, 32a.

127. Plato, *Gorgias*, 474a.

128. *Gorgias*, 509a.

129. Aristotle, *Magna Moralia*, 2.6.1200 B 75, in Ferguson, *Socrates*, p 182; Diogenes Laertius, *Life of Socrates*, in Ferguson, *Socrates*, p 25.

130. C C W Taylor, in *Socrates* (OUP, Oxford: 1998) p 27, points to Milton's Satan as an example of someone willingly embracing evil and draws the inference that 'He [Socrates] seems never to have met a fallen man, let alone a fallen angel'. Satan as an existential hero, though, is following Socrates and doing what he thinks is right from his deepest heart's being and, given the way many readers of *Paradise Lost* respond positively to Satan's rebelliousness and sympathise with his cause, the possibility that Satan is good cannot simply be denied. Hitler might seem to be a better example of willed nastiness but, Socrates might say, his behaviour was rooted in ignorance.

131. Diogenes Laertius, *Socrates*, 40, in Ferguson, *Socrates*, p 27.

132. Diogenes Laertius, *Socrates*, 41, in Ferguson, *Socrates*, p 27. Plato, *Apology*, 17c.

133. Plato, *Apology*, 19b.

134. Plato, *Apology*, 20e.

135. Plato, *Apology*, 22d.

136. Plato, *Apology*, 23d.

137. Plato, *Apology*, 26c.

138. Plato, *Apology*, 18c.

139. Plutarch, *Plutarch's Lives,* 'Life of Nicias', p 189. E R Dodds, *The Greeks and the Irrational* (University of California Press, Berkeley and Los Angeles: 1951) p 189. The case put by Dodds has been contested: see I F Stone, *The Trial of Socrates*, pp 230–47.

140. Plato, *Apology*, 27c.

141. Plato, *Apology*, 28a–b.

142. Plato, *Apology*, 28d.

143. Plato, *Apology*, 28e.

144. Plato, *Apology*, 29e–30a.

145. Plato, *Apology*, 33a.

146. Xenophon, *Defence of Socrates*, from *The Complete Works of Xenophon*, p 514 and p 515. Socrates' unwillingness to go on living is also expressed at the end of Xenophon, *Memoirs*, 4.7.

147. Plato, *Apology*, 36e.

148. Plato, *Apology*, 39d.

149. Plato, *Apology*, 40c–d.

150. Plato, *Apology*, 41e.

151. Plato, *Apology*, 42.

152. Plato's *Apology* begins, *I do not know, men of Athens, how my accusers affected you.*

153. Plato, *Phaedo*, 118a.

154. Xenophon, *Memoirs*, 4.7, p 599.

155. For Socrates' influence on Hellenistic and Roman philosophy, see Pierre Hadot, *Philosophy as a Way of Life*.

156. Seneca, *Letters* 28.2 and *On Anger*, 3.11.2 in Ferguson, *Socrates*, p 195 and p 196.

157. 'What does Socrates treat more amply than himself? And what does he most often lead his pupils to do, if not to talk about themselves – not about what they have read in their books but about the being and movement of their souls?' Michel De Montaigne, *The Complete Essays* (Penguin Books, London: 2003) p 425.

158. Quoted in Nehemas, *The Art of Living*, p 114.

159. Quoted in Hadot, *Philosophy as a Way of Life*, p 157.

160. Søren Kierkegaard, *Concluding Unscientific Postscript to the Philosophical Fragments* from Michael Watts, *Kierkegaard* (Oneworld, Oxford: 2003) p 81.

161. Kierkegaard, *Concluding Unscientific Postscript to the Philosophical Fragments*, from Watts, p 87.

162. Ferguson, *Socrates* p 21 and Friedrich Nietzsche, *The Birth of Tragedy* (Oxford University Press, Oxford: 2000) p 73.

163. Nietzsche, *The Birth of Tragedy*, 13.

164. This is the concern of chapter five of Alexander Nehamas, *The Art of Living*.

165. Friedrich Nietzsche, *Beyond Good and Evil* (Penguin, London: 2003) p 32.

166. From notes by Nietzsche for an unfinished essay, quoted in Nehamas, *The Art of Living*, p 132.

167. Nietzsche, *The Birth of Tragedy*, 13.

168. Friedrich Nietzsche, *Twilight of the Idols*, 9 (Penguin, London: 1974) p 33.

169. Section 15 of Nietzsche, *The Birth of Tragedy*.

170. Nietzsche, *The Birth of Tragedy*, 15.

171. Nietzsche, *The Birth of Tragedy*, 15.

172. Xenophon, *Banquet*, 2, from *The Complete Works of Xenophon*, p 606.

173. Nietzsche, *Beyond Good and Evil*, 212.

174. Plato, *Crito*, 48b.

175. Plato, *Crito*, 46b.

176. Plato, *Apology*, 41b. Palamedes was framed by Odysseus and made to appear a traitor at Troy, a charge for which he was executed by his own army. Odysseus had forged a letter from Priam, the Trojan king, implicating Palamedes as a traitor willing to betray the Greeks for gold. Odysseus did this, and hid gold in Palamedes' tent to incriminate him further, as an act of revenge because it was Palamedes who had detected his stratagem for trying to avoid service in Troy by pretending to be mad.

177. Quoted in Pankaj Mishra, *An End to Suffering: The Buddha in the World* (Picador, London: 2004) p 191.

178. See Mishra, *An End to Suffering*, pp 380–7.

179. Georges Friedman, *La Puissance et la sagesse*, translated by Pierre Hadot and quoted in his *Philosophy as a Way of Life*, p 70.

180. Plato, *Apology*, 38.

Year	Age	Life
470/ 469		Birth of Socrates.
461	9	Pericles rises to power in Athens.
458	12	Building of Long Walls connecting port of Piraeus to Athens begins.
454	16	Treasury of the Delian League moved to Athens.
450	20	Birth of Alcibiades.
447	23	Building of Parthenon begins.
432	38	Siege of Potidaea by Athens begins: Socrates serves there. Parthenon completed.
431	39	Outbreak of Peloponnesian War. Thucydides begins writing his *History of the Peloponnesian War*. Pericles gives his funeral oration. Sparta invades Attica.
430	40	Surrender of Potidaea. Plague in Athens. Birth of Xenophon. Chaerephon journeys to Delphi to ask the oracle if anyone is wiser than his friend Socrates.
429	41	Death of Pericles.
428	42	Island of Lesbos, lead by the city of Mytilene, rebels against Athens.
427	43	Capture of Mytilene by Athens and executions of rebels. Birth of Plato.
425	45	Athenians capture Sphacteria.

Year	History	Culture
470/ 469		
461		
458	Cinnicinatus appointed Dictator of Rome and defeats the Aequi.	Aeschylus, *Orestia*.
454	Greeks in Egypt defeated by Persian Satrap Megabyzus.	
450	Romans take Greek city of Tarentum in Italy.	Birth of Aristophanes.
447	Revolt of Megabyzus, Persian Satrap of Syria.	Death of the poet Pindar.
432		
431		Euripedes, *Medea*.
430		
429		
427		
425		

Year	Age	Life
424	46	Athenians invade Boeotia: Socrates present at Athenian defeat at Delium. Spartan general Brasidas takes Amphipolis in Northern Greece.
423	47	One-year armistice between Athens and Sparta.
422	48	Socrates serves at battle of Amphipolis, where Brasidas and Cleon are both killed.
421	49	Peace of Nicias.
416	54	Massacre at Melos by the Athenians.
415	55	Mutilation of the herms in Athens. Athenian expedition to Sicily. Alcibiades flees to Sparta.
413	57	Athenian army in Sicily defeated.
412	58	Island of Chios rebels against Athens.
411	59	Oligarchic revolution in Athens and Council of 400 established.
410	60	Democratic rule restored in Athens. Athenian fleet under Alcibiades defeats Spartans at battle of Cyzicus.
407	63	Alcibiades returns from exile.
406	64	Athenian defeat at Notium. Athenians defeat Spartan fleet at Arginusae: Socrates opposes subsequent charges against Athenian generals for failure to aid damaged Athenian ships.
405	65	Battle of Aegospotami: Athenian fleet defeated by Sparta. Piraeus blockaded and Athens besieged by Sparta.
404	66	Athens surrenders to Spartans and rule of the Thirty imposed. Death of Alcibiades.

Year	History	Culture
424	Xerxes II, King of Persia, assassinated and succeeded by Darius II.	Death of the historian Herodotus.
423		Aristophanes' *Clouds* performed at Athens
422		
421		Aristophanes' *Peace* performed at Athens.
416		
415		Euripedes, *The Trojan Women*.
413		
412		
411		
410		
407		Euripedes, *Iphigenia in Aulis*.
406	Dionysus I becomes Tyrant of Syracuse.	Death of Euripedes. Death of Sophocles.
405	Death of Darius II of Persia: succeeded by Artaxerxes II.	Aristophanes' *Frogs* performed at Athens.
404		

Year	Age	Life
403	67	Fall of the Thirty: democracy restored in Athens.
401	69	Xenophon joins expedition of the 'Ten Thousand' to Asia.
399	70	Trial and execution of Socrates.

Year	History	Culture
403		
401		
399		

Further Reading

Plato

Socrates wrote no philosophical works but a number of early texts by Plato are read as reflecting the thought of Socrates. These texts are known as the Socratic dialogues and the principal ones with respect to Socrates' life are the *Apology* and the *Crito*. The other texts that most scholars regard as Socratic dialogues include *Charmides, Euthyphro, Gorgias, Hippias Minor, Ion, Laches, Meno* and *Protagoras*. There are also a number of texts belonging to Plato's middle period which feature Socrates as the major character. These are principally the *Phaedo, Symposium, Parmenides* and *Theaetetus.*

All these texts are in *Plato Complete Works*, edited by John M Cooper (Hackett, Indianapolis: 1997) and the book's introduction includes a lucid discussion of the vexed question of which texts constitute the Socratic dialogues and the related question of the chronological versus thematic groupings of Plato's works.

In the Oxford World's Classics series, Plato's *Defence of Socrates* (another name for the *Apology*), *Euthyphro* and *Crito* are usefully available in one book, translated by David Gallop (Oxford University Press, Oxford: 1999). Plato, *Symposium* (Oxford University Press, Oxford: 1998), translated by Robin Waterfield, and Plato, *Protagoras* (Oxford University Press, Oxford: 2002), translated by C C W Taylor are in the same series.

Plato, *The Last Days of Socrates*, translated by Hugh Tredennick and edited by Harold Tarrant (Penguin, London: 2003) contains *Euthyphro*, *Apology*, *Crito* and *Phaedo*. Plato, *The Symposium* (Penguin, London: 2003) is also available.

Xenophon

The most accessible collection of Xenophon's works about Socrates is Xenophon, *Conversations of Socrates* (Penguin, London: 1990). This contains *The Defence of Socrates*, *Memoirs*, *The Dinner Party* (*Banquet/Symposium*) and *Estate Management*.

Aristophanes

There are many editions of Aristophanes' *Clouds*, the play featuring Socrates, including Aristophanes, *Clouds*, translated by Peter Meineck (Hackett, Indianapolis: 2000), and Aristophanes *Lysistrata*, *The Acharnians*, *The Clouds*, translated by Alan H Sommerstein (Penguin, London: 1973).

Ancient sources

John Ferguson*, Socrates A Source Book* (Macmillan, London: 1970) is a collection in English of ancient source material on Socrates. It includes full translations of Plato's *Apology* and *Crito*, selections from other Plato texts and selections from Xenophon and Aristophanes. What makes the book especially valuable, though, are the selections of writing on Socrates from Diogenes Laertius, Aristotle, Cicero, Plutarch and a host of later writers.

Historical and social background

Boardman, John, Jasper Griffin and Oswyn Murray (eds), *The Oxford History of Greece and the Hellenistic World* (Oxford University Press, Oxford: 1991). Authoritative accounts of the historical and cultural background to the life and times of Socrates.

Cartledge, Paul, *The Cambridge Illustrated History of Ancient Greece* (Cambridge University Press, Cambridge: 1998). Nine experts in their fields writing about classical Greek culture in a refreshing style. The book is richly illustrated in colour.

Kagan, Donald, *The Peloponnesian War* (Harper Perennial, London: 2005). A detailed but very readable account of the conflict between Athens and Sparta.

Modern studies

Brickhouse, Thomas C, and Nicholas D Smith (eds), *Plato and the Trial of Socrates* (Routledge, New York and London: 2004). A title in the Routledge Philosophy Guidebook series, this is a guide for philosophy students to the *Euthyphro, Apology, Crito* and the death scene from *Phaedo*. Detailed interpretations of the texts, sometimes too closely argued for the general reader, but well worth consulting for particular passages.

Colaiaco, James A, *Socrates against Athens* ((Routledge, New York and London: 2001). A good general account of the trial that pits philosophy against the state and with due regard for the social and cultural background.

Forstater, Mark, *The Living Wisdom of Socrates* (Hodder and Stoughton, London: 2004). A book for the general reader about the way Socrates continues to exert an influence on our reflections about the modern world.

Guthrie, W K C, *Socrates* (Cambridge University Press, Cambridge: 1971). A readable, scholarly study that covers the Socrates problem and the life, character and philosophy of Socrates. It was first published as the second part of Guthrie's *A History of Greek Philosophy* (Cambridge University Press, Cambridge: 1969).

Hadot, Pierre, *Philosophy as a Way of Life* (Blackwell, Oxford: 2000). An absorbing account of the history of spiritual exercises in antiquity and with a chapter devoted to Socrates.

Nehamas, Alexander, *The Art of Living* (University of California Press, Berkeley/Los Angeles/London: 2000). Thoughts on

Socrates and a series of Socratic reflections on the work of Montaigne, Nietzsche and Foucault. An exceptional and endearing book in more than one way and highly recommended.

Reeve, C D C, *Socrates in the Apology* (Hackett, Indianapolis: 1989). A detailed interpretation of Plato's *Apology* with a view to reaching an understanding of Socrates as he appears in that text. The style of writing is admirably accessible and amenable to readers with various backgrounds and interests.

Stone, I F, *The Trial of Socrates* (Pimlico, London: 1997). A provocative and highly partial account of the trial by a campaigning journalist, portraying Socrates as an illiberal and arrogant anti-democrat. Some of the scholarship has been questioned and Stone overplays his case.

Taylor, A E, *Socrates* (Peter Davies Limited, London: 1932). Out of date in some respects but still a good read on the life and philosophy of Socrates.

Taylor, C C W *Socrates* (Oxford University Press, Oxford: 1998). A lucid introduction to the life and philosophy of Socrates.

Vlastos, Gregory, *Socrates: Ironist and Moral Philosopher* (Cambridge University Press, Cambridge: 1991). A renowned Socrates scholar writing for an academic audience.

Pictures Sources

The author and publishers wish to express their thanks to the following sources of illustrative material and/or permission to reproduce it. They will make the proper acknowledgements in future editions in the event that any omissions have occurred.

akg-Images: p. 33; Getty Images: pp. 3, 5, 19, 29, 39, 57, 68, 95, 97, 102, 108; Topham Picturepoint: pp. 25, 37, 48, 78.

Index

CLEOPATRA

Cleopatra VII (69–30 BC) Egyptian queen (of Macedonian descent), last ruler of the Ptolemaic dynasty in Egypt. Daughter of Ptolemy XII, she ruled with her two brother-husbands, Ptolemy XIII and Ptolemy XIV, both of whom she had killed, and with her son Ptolemy XV or Caesarion (44–30).

This biography concentrates on the fascinating aspect of Cleopatra's ever-shifting identity. A master of self-presentation, she was the first to craft for herself an image or, to be precise, a number of images. Depending on the audience, she might present herself as a goddess, a political leader, or an alluring and exotic woman. Roman statesmen likewise manipulated Cleopatra's image for their own political ends. The tension embodied in our sources for Cleopatra's life make her story especially captivating.

The author's approach to the biography focuses on the ancient sources, both the historical – Plutarch, Suetonius, Cassius Dio, Julius Caesar, Appian, and Velleius Paterculus – and the literary – Horace, Virgil and Lucan. Documentary evidence from inscriptions also is important. In addition, texts like Cicero's Letters provides some real-time snapshots of Cleopatra.

Contents: Preface – The Ptolemies of Egypt – The Young Cleopatra – Caesar and Cleopatra in Alexandria – Cleopatra in Rome – Antony and Cleopatra in Tarsus – The Inimitable Life – Fulvia and Octavia – The Donations of Alexandria – The War of Words – Actium – Inseparable in Death – The Fate of Egypt – *Notes – Chronology – Sources and Further Reading – Picture Sources – Index*

Prudence Jones is Assistant Professor at Montclair State University, having graduated from Harvard University with a Ph.D. in Classical Philology in 1999. She has lectured widely on Cleopatra, including at the APA Annual Meeting in Dallas in 1999. She is the author of a Cleopatra: A Sourcebook as well as articles in journals, such as Classical World and Latomus.

Paperback
978-1-904950-25-7
UK £10.99/US $15.95
160 Pages, illustrated in colour, map, 198 × 128 mm, Ancient History

ALEXANDER THE GREAT

Alexander the Great

Alexander the Great (356–323 BC), King of Macedonia, lived a life of mythical proportions. He modelled himself on Achilles and slept with a copy of the *Iliad*, annotated by Aristotle, his teacher, under his pillow. Unrivalled by any historical military figure, he conquered the Mediterranean, Persia, Afghanistan and northwest India during his brief life. By the time he died at the age of 33 he had introduced Greek civilisation to the world. A gifted strategist and self-proclaimed deity, Alexander was impetuous and merciless in warfare. He never lost a battle. Exhibiting conspicuous personal bravery, two millenia after his death he is still remembered as the greatest soldier of all times.

Contents: The Man Who Would Be King – Cutting the Gordian Knot – The Great King of Persia – The Invasion of Egypt – The Spoils of War – Lord of Asia – Across the Hindu Kush – The Persian Wedding – Into India – Victory on the Hydaspes – Turning Homeward – The Purge of Persia – Death in Babylon – *Notes – Chronology – Sources and Further Reading – Picture Sources – Index*

Nigel Cawthorne has written many books and his work has appeared in newspapers on both sides of the Atlantic.

Paperback
978-1-904950-56-7
UK £9.99/US $15.95
186 Pages, illustrated in colour, map, 198 × 128 mm, Ancient History

By the same author:
Julius Caesar
Paperback
978-1-904950-11-0
UK £9.99/US $14.95

LIFE&TIMES
PHILOSOPHY

SARTRE

'It helps the reader understand where, under particular historical and political pressures, intellectuals in a certain tradition went wrong, or got things right. It offers a measured and detailed summary of the ways in which Sartre, his allies, their opponents and some of their successors intervened in political debates, from the purge of collaborators after liberation up to the attempted purge of sans papiers in the 1990s.' *Times Literary Supplement*

Jean-Paul Sartre (1905–1980) dominated the cultural and literary life of post-war France.

He believed from an early age that he had a mission to be a writer and proceeded to realise this as a novelist, philosopher, screenwriter, playwright, literary and art critic, biographer, essayist, polemicist and journalist. Although before the Second World War Sartre showed little inclination to become involved in politics, from 1945 he established himself as the very personification of intellectual commitment, taking public positions on national and international political issues from the Liberation until very shortly before his death. In this new biography, published by Haus to mark the centenary of Sartre's birth, David Drake considers the works of France's most famous 20th century intellectual, his relations with his contemporaries, notably his life-long companion Simone de Beauvoir, fellow novelist and playwright Albert Camus and sociologist Raymond Aron, and the political causes he espoused, all of which the author firmly locates in the turbulent times through which Sartre lived.

Contents: Introduction – Early Years (1905–1924) – From the École Normale to the Outbreak of the War (1924–1939) – *The War Really Divided My Life in Two* (1939–1944)- Existentialism and Communism (1944–1950) – *An Anticommunist is a Rat* (1950–1956) – Marxism and Anti-colonialism (1956–1967) – May 1968, Maoism and Flaubert (1967–1980) – Conclusion – *Notes* – *Chronology* – *Further Reading* – *Index*

David Drake, Principal Lecturer in French at Middlesex University, London, is President of the United Kingdom Society for Sartrean Studies (UKSSS) and a member of the Editorial Board of Sartre Studies International and of Modern and Contemporary France.

Paperback

978-1-904341-85-7

UK £9.99 / US $16.95

194 Pages, illustrated in colour, 197 × 127 mm, Philosophy and French History

SIMONE DE BEAUVOIR

Simone de Beauvoir (1908–1986) always stood in the shadow of her lover and teacher, Jean Paul Sartre, despite the fact that she was a brilliant writer and philosopher in her own right. She described their unique partnership as 'the one undoubted success in my life'. It is, however, her monumental study *The Second Sex* and her four-volume autobiography which made her a cult figure of the Feminist movement. Above everything in her writing and political activism, she valued her own intellectual honesty.

Lisa Appignanesi is a novelist, writer and broadcaster. She has written a portrait of *Simone de Beauvoir and Cabaret* (2004, Yale University Press) and a book on James, Proust and Musil. She is the co-author of *Freud's Women* with John Forrester (Penguin).

Paperback
978-1-904950-09-7
UK £9.99/US $16.95
182 Pages, illustrated in colour, 198 × 128 mm, Gender & Women's Studies and Philosophy